THE I

Finding Faith Th

by
Halbert Katzen, J.D.

Insights Out Publishing

The Logic of Love
Finding Faith through the Heart-Mind Connection

By Halbert Katzen, J.D.

Published by:

Insights Out Publishing

Insights Out Publishing
P.O. Box 11286
Boulder, CO 80301 U.S.A.

Homer and Non Sequitur ~ 1999, The Washington Post Writers Group. Reprinted with permission.

Dave's Wyrd © 1998 David Chastain. Reprinted with permission.

Printed in the United States of America

Publisher's Cataloging-in-Publication
(Provided by Quality Books, Inc.)

Katzen, Halbert.
    The logic of love : finding faith through the heart-mind connection / by Halbert Katzen. -- 1st ed.
        p. cm.
        LCCN: 99-95212
        ISBN: 0-9672949-7-5

        1. Theism. 2. Faith. 3. God--Love. 4. Love--Religious aspects.
    I. Title

BL200.K38 1999   212
                                 QBI99-913

DEDICATION
✦ ✦ ✦

This book is dedicated to the reader,
each and every one of you. Bless your hearts.

ACKNOWLEDGEMENTS
✦ ✦ ✦

Special thanks goes to those who
generously gave their time by providing me
with feedback during the process of writing
this book. They are: Hirsh and Melissa Katzen,
Cristina Seaborn, Mike Boileau, Dave
Williamson III, Scott "Gypsy" Greene, JoiLin
Johnson, Bari Boyer, Carol Setters, and Nicole
Bruckner.

I would also like to thank the professionals
who worked with me on this project. For
editing: Paul Griffin, Jasmin Cori, and Jody
Berman. Cover design and printing
coordination: Orbit Design. Page layout and
interior graphics: Char Campbell.

TABLE OF CONTENTS

✦ ✦ ✦

TABLE OF CONTENTS

✦ ✦ ✦

PROLOGUE

✦ ✦ ✦

The dress code at Phillips Exeter Academy required coats and ties above the waist, but permitted jeans, even shorts, below the waist. This administratively adopted schizophrenic approach to apparel represented an attempt at balancing Ivy League intellects with adolescent bodies. The academics were advanced and the facilities were fantastic, but aside from that, it had all the same social dynamics as any other high school in America.

Culturally speaking, Exeter was the epitome of preppy, and anyone who broke out of this stereotype assumed certain risks. Adolescence, of course, provided a heaping helping of ostracism for deviants. But attendance at Exeter was supposed to be a ticket to the good life. So, the price of nonconformity had a premium attached. Nonconformity was blasphemy because it meant a rare opportunity was being foolishly squandered. We were being prepared for corporate culture. The name of the game was *Coloring Within The Lines*.

Consequently, an expectation of the ordinary pervaded the student body whenever student council presidential candidates gave their campaign speeches. Our highest hope was to be amused. This usually came in the form of watching a peer sweat under the pressure of public speaking. They tried their best to be compelling, and we tried our best to be polite. The only thing out of the ordinary the year my classmates were running was that Scott Greene sat on stage, waiting his turn.

Scott was not your typical student. There was nothing preppy about him. His hair was long. He often wore it under a bandanna tied gypsy style. That's why Scott had been affectionately nicknamed *Gypsy*. To those of us who knew him, he was a bright light of kindness. But as a candidate in this race, he was a dark horse indeed.

When it was Scott's turn to speak, we could see immediately that his agenda was bigger than the election. He was writhing with excitement and consumed with passion.

Neither protocol nor preparation could shepherd him through the experience. With a certain degree of reluctance, he apparently allowed a desperate muse to enter his body. He seemed both possessed and self-aware.

At first, he tried to use the microphone. Then, he apologetically cut loose from the tether and, stepping away from the lectern, made sure that his natural voice could reach the ears of all those present. Unprotected by the lectern's safe harbor, he began tacking back and forth across the breadth of the stage. We all watched in amazement as Scott sailed forth with a plea for a student body dedicated to the values of love, honesty, and forgiveness. He spoke briefly on the importance of these values as they related to student life and ended his talk by affirming that his purpose was to deliver the message, not to get elected. In less than one minute he accomplished what he had set out to do. So, with touching humility, he thanked us for indulging him and returned to his seat.

Scott won, and I learned something. Love transforms the individual and transcends cultural differences. It empowers people and unifies communities. Love accomplishes more than it sets out to do; it is the self-created miracle in our lives. Scott's election inspired hope and revealed the good in others. I had never witnessed a friend take such an extraordinary stand for love. His willingness to do so opened the doors of opportunity wider than imagination.

There is a direct connection between that day and this book. Scott was a catalyst for helping me focus on what I had been striving to create in my life. He took the ethereal sentiments of the heart and crystallized them into expressible values. His courage was inspirational and his election affirmed the transformational power of love. On that day I learned that with love, anything is possible.

Thanks, Scott.

Introduction

✦ ✦ ✦

The Logic of Love is written for those who embrace love—the desire and willingness to do well for others—as the most important value in life. The tools of logic are used to fabricate a paradigm of spiritual family from the material of commonly shared experiences. This structure is held together with love.

The Logic of Love demonstrates how faith in God *can be* a logical extension of love. If you do not have faith in God, this book offers an approach to faith that does not play upon your emotions or ask you to believe testimonials. In fact, it is written from an agnostic perspective. If you do have faith, but have trouble communicating to others that this is reasonable, the ideas presented here can help you express your faith to others as a logical and loving approach to life. This is a conversation about spirituality that is based on nothing more than love and freewill. It is not about trying to prove the existence of God. It is about exploring the possibilities and making a choice.

My challenge is to use words such as *love, God*, and *faith* in a clear and consistent manner. Though there is nothing unusual about how I define these terms, for most people these words are loaded with layers of personal meaning. We create individual definitions for words relating to spirituality because these words reflect our own understanding of life. Given the diversity of spiritual experience, we naturally allow words to take on various shades of meanings. For now, please accept the way I use these terms. My goal is not to create crystallized definitions designed to transcend time. It is only to show how holding love as the highest value can logically support faith in God.

This book presents an internally consistent theistic paradigm and considers which of the three gnostic paradigms—atheism, agnosticism or theism—best complements the value of love. It provides a foundation for understanding that faith in God is not only a reasonable choice, but also a choice that is a logical outgrowth of love. The internal consistency of atheistic and agnostic paradigms is assumed and, therefore, will not be explored in depth.

Valid reasons exist that admonish us to approach the subject of faith cautiously. Life is filled with what seems like needless suffering. Atrocities are, and always have been, committed in the name of God. Religions have failed to co-exist peacefully with each other. Superficially, the condition of our planet suggests that we do not enjoy the loving care of an all-powerful, all-knowing God. There are reasons that make faith in God look like a bad idea. But, *if* love is espoused as the highest value in life, *then* I believe we can find even better reasons for having faith. This is what I would like to share with you.

PART I

DEFINING LOVE, LOGIC, FREEWILL, AND GOD

✦ ✦ ✦

The beginning of wisdom is the definition of terms.
Socrates

✦ ✦ ✦

Part I lays a foundation for understanding the terms *love, logic, freewill*, and *God*. Combing these concepts into a context is the critical issue. The context provides structure for appreciating the meaning of these terms. The last chapter interrelates these concepts to show how proof of God's existence would work to undermine our ability to freely choose love. It shows why we can't have our cake and eat it too. This sets the stage for Part II, an appreciation for the special nature of spiritual faith.

LOVE

✦ ✦ ✦

I love sports
My dog loves me
I love my country
And my family

I love God and
My neighborhood
I love to think I'm
Doing what I should

I love you
And I love me
And I love . . .I love
Let me see . . .

✦ ✦ ✦

Love is the desire and willingness to do well for others. Love is alive when it is embraced as a personal value, as an attitude put into action. We will focus on appreciating it as a self-empowered choice, as compared to experiencing it as an emotion.

The premise is that love is the highest value in our lives.

This is our starting point; *everything* rests on this assumption. By "the highest value," I mean that all other values are relative and situation-specific compared to the primacy of love. Values such as honesty, fairness, mercy, loyalty, affection, or peace are important because they are the colors into which the white light of love becomes refracted as it shines through the prism of our individual experience. Sometimes these subordinate values compete with each other for positions of relative importance, but the assumption is that they cannot compete with the supreme value of love. For example, speaking the truth is important. Yet it is a value that is regularly sacrificed for the sake of love:

> "Where are we going for dinner?" asks Girlfriend on her birthday.
> "I got us the best table at that restaurant on top of the World Trade Center," says Boyfriend, beaming with pride.
> Yet when the elevator stops a few floors below the top and opens on a surprise party, everybody is smiling as Girlfriend compliments Boyfriend on his ruse.

Girlfriend is happy because too much honesty can spoil love. The value of truth was never intended to ruin a surprise party.

As well, truth should never be an excuse for cruelty:

> "How do you like my hat?" asks Miss I. M. Insecure.

---

[1]After my son, Jaron, was conceived, I became especially frustrated with the English language. The lack of an androgynous pronoun made it impossible for me to address this developing child appropriately. I was loath to refer to him as "it." Not knowing whether I was to become the father of a son or daughter, "he" and "she" seemed inappropriate. Eventually, I came to the conclusion

"I think it's the most ridiculous piece of
apparel you've worn in the past decade, and in
your case, that's no easy feat to accomplish,"
snaps Mr. B. Little.

Just because someone may prefer the undiluted, graceless
truth in all circumstances, hopefully che[1] does not try to
justify making others feel like a steaming pile of poop just

---

that the only reason why there are no androgynous pronouns is
because as a culture we are slothful and haphazard when it comes
to progressively developing our language. This slothfulness undermines our ability to think and communicate clearly. Contemporary
writers have been awkwardly trying to deal with the situation by
using "s/he" or using "he" in one chapter and "she" in the next.
Similar frustrations have come up for writers who want to use a
pronoun for God that is personal but androgynous.

We can do better. Please join with me in using the following
new words so that we can put an end to this age-long problem.
Who put us in charge of such a task, you ask? At the very least, we
have the silent consent from all those before us and around us who
have forsaken this responsibility.

So, here they are (Can we have a drum roll, please!?!):

Che: (pronounced like "cheek" without the "k") an androgynous specific pronoun as compared to the androgynous, unspecific
pronoun "one."

Chen: (pronounced like "check" but with an "n") the direct
object of the androgynous, specific pronoun che. Chen is an
androgynous substitute for *him* and *her*.

Chens: the possessive form of chen. As with his and hers, the
possessive form is spelled without an apostrophe.

Chenself: the reflexive form of chen.

At first the use and sound of these words may seem awkward.
This is because 1) we have so long denied ourselves the ability to
express these thoughts, and 2) new words by their nature tend to have
an unfamiliar ring to them. Short new words can be especially odd
sounding because so many of the combinations of sounds for short
words have already been used. In time, however, with regular use
and the willingness to share these words with others, they will slip
into our thoughts and expressions as unnoticed as the air we breathe.

because they do not have the same thick skin that protects the vigilant defender of Unbridled-Truth-In-All-Circumstances. "Do unto others as you would have them do unto you," when taken too literally, means imposing one's personal prioritization of the values that are subordinate to love. However, if the "do" in "Do unto others" means *love others as they are best loved*, then this principle can truly be a reflection of prioritizing the value of love. With love leading the way, we can come up with many creative ways of "doing unto others" that are neither insensitive to, nor catering to, another's weaknesses.

With love as the highest value, the importance of truth becomes relative. Sometimes it is easy to appreciate when we should sacrifice truth for the sake of love. The above examples were used to make this as black and white as possible. Of course, life is filled with gray areas as well. Here comes Joe Gray, now. Let's see if we can solve his problem.

> "Should I tell my spouse that I cheated?" pleads Mr. Gray. "I feel so bad. I'm sure it will never happen again. Should I burden her with the truth? If I don't tell her, maybe I'll end up being less judgmental of her. We could end up having a much better relationship in the long run."

Sorry, Joe, but don't look for an answer here. This is not *Rationalizations 101*. Nor is it about creating some kind of decision-tree for instant application to all the sordid situations in which we may find ourselves. The point here is that all too often in life, when times get tough, a value other than love (such as truth) becomes the standard for measuring human worth. Maybe for that particular situation it is appropriate, and maybe it isn't. But if it is, then this is because *that* value is the best reflection of love in *that* particular situation. Tomorrow's problems may be different.

As long as love is the highest value, we are far less likely to be viewed by others or ourselves as two-faced hypocrites when the next situation calls for a reprioritization of the values that are subordinate to love. Love is a chameleon. Sometimes its color is honesty; sometimes it is loyalty; sometimes it is keeping or breaking a promise. And sometimes love may be expressed by eating dinner.

Do we eat to live or live to eat? I hope that every morsel of food that passes through our lips is succulent and juicy. May we never be rushed through a single meal. May there always be enough to give us that comfortably satisfied feeling. And above all, may we come to understand that our appreciation of the good things in life, and our pursuit of them, does not necessarily make us a bunch of selfish sinners who should be ashamed for not having a higher commitment to love.

I am not here to say how we should strike the balance between engaging in activities that are directly serviceable to others and taking "down time." Replenishing our physical, mental, and spiritual bodies is essential if we are to have the energy to love others directly. But I do wish to promote the idea that even when replenishing, we can appreciate such experiences as extensions of our commitment to love.

Whether we should have given that money to the poor rather than having stuffed ourselves with steak and lobster last night is a level of micromanagement on which I wish us all the best of luck. Unfortunately, some of us can only dream of being plagued by such "tough" decisions. The intent of this book is to inspire us to make decisions that define our spiritual lives so that love flows more easily. Love does not flow easily when our stomachs are empty, when we are experiencing the preoccupation that comes with too much stress or, in the most extreme case, when we are dead. Although there may be times in life when we truly are called upon to die for love, this does not mean we should set about killing ourselves for love. Though it may be difficult to clearly define the ceiling of excessive living, we should at

least be comfortable with our feet firmly planted on the floor
of necessities.

Understanding and appreciating this difference can help
create the inner peace that inspires commitment to the value
of love. Living love is far more important than
understanding love, yet an understanding of love can
certainly help us to better live by this value. On the subject of
love, Lou Reed once sang, "Between thought and expression
there lies a lifetime." Clarifying our thoughts about love
provides us an opportunity to express it better.

The Logic of Love should not be read with the intention of
trying to achieve and maintain an emotional state of bliss.
Naturally, if loving other people feels good, this supports the
value of love. I do not mean to turn a deaf ear to the issue of
emotions. However, such is the tail, not the dog. Love may
indeed generate the broadest range and deepest levels of
emotional satisfaction. But bear in mind that this book will
be most beneficial to the reader who has an eye toward being
of service to others, rather than on achieving emotional
consolation for oneself. Attitude is everything. If emotional
satisfaction is seen as the bonus, not the goal, then you will
stand the best chance of appreciating my intended meaning.

Defining love as the desire and willingness to do well for
others is the easy part. Shedding the emotional baggage that
can drag down our appreciation of love is a lifelong process.
Balancing the giving with the receiving is love's challenge to
us all. Prioritizing the values that are subordinate to love is
the art of living. My hope is that this book will make the
process, art, and challenge of living a bit easier.

Reasoning and Experience

✦ ✦ ✦

Mr. Mindfull thought he had it
    All figured out, but when
He took one step out his front door,
    He came back in again.
The weatherman had said quite clearly
    There was no chance of rain.
So when he felt some drops come down
    They hit him in the brain.

Since he was blind, he could not see.
    And the cars made such a bleat,
He could not hear the sprinklers
    Which were ten yards from his feet.
So, neither the weatherman's wisdom,
    Nor the experience of the street,
Provided him the answer.
    But still, ain't life a treat!

✦ ✦ ✦

When considering whether faith in God is a logical extension of love, we quite naturally turn to logic as a tool for exploring the question. But it is only one of the fabulous tools at our disposal. Intuitive reasoning and experience also play an important role in developing an answer to such a profound question. We can interrelate our experiences with our logical and intuitive reasoning abilities. This enhances our ability to reach decisions that make the most of our experiences and reflect our best thinking.

Our understanding and appreciation of life comes from two main sources: reasoning and experience. The interplay between the inner world of reasoning and the outer world of experience provides an opportunity for each realm to improve the other. We use our reasoning abilities to interpret our experiences and give them meaning. We construct meanings and apply values in an effort to appreciate what has already occurred. These interpretations of past experience can then be used as storehouses of wisdom to make better decisions in the present. In this way our reasoning works to both interpret and direct our experiences. There is a continuous feedback loop between reasoning and experience for the development of insight.

Reasoning and experience, however, are sometimes in conflict with each other. For example, a sprinkler can make us think it is raining. When there is conflict, then our experience has been misinterpreted and/or our reasoning process is faulty. Working to keep reasoning and experience in harmony can provide a sense of security about our understanding of life.

There can also be disharmony between logic and intuition—the two modes of reasoning. When this is the case, it indicates that we have not yet developed our best wisdom on an issue. Insights developed with logic are often respected more than insights gleaned through intuition. In fact, some definitions of intuition place this faculty of the mind outside the realm of reason. However, the value of direct perception—intuition—is *not* inferior to logical reasoning. What gives rise to the devaluation of intuition is a tendency to use it in situations that call for logical reasoning.

Intuitive reasoning is appropriately applied when time is

of the essence, when decisions are too close to call, or when the need to make a decision does not require the use of logic. Keen intuitive insights are labeled "brilliant," and the seers of such insights commonly get showered with accolades. This reflects our general appreciation for well-developed intuitive abilities.

Unfortunately, intuition can easily become confused with other internal experiences, such as emotions. Sometimes it can be difficult to distinguish a "gut feeling" from gas caused by the burrito we had for dinner. Those who are familiar with the original *Star Trek* television series may recall how the show regularly poked fun at Mr. Spock, an alien crew member. Mr. Spock's native culture glorified logic and shunned emotion. Because he inappropriately equated emotion with intuition, Spock would awkwardly stammer through situations that called for quick decisions, educated guesses, or personal preferences.

Intuitive reasoning does have a down side. The problem, however, is not that it is rooted in emotion; the "problem" is that the cognitive process underlying intuition is unarticulable because it tends toward spontaneity. When the Logician is confronted, the question "Why?" gets a "because" with stuff after it. When the Intuitor is confronted with the same question, there is no stuff after the "because." Just because. When we do not need to explain ourselves to anyone else, then "just because" is just fine. But when we have the time and want to *reason together*, then logic is the form of reasoning that can be shared. Logic gives us the opportunity to scrutinize and critique our ideas and insights. Through this process, we can progressively develop common understandings that help us live in harmony with each other. Logic can be a powerful, unifying force.

As with intuition, logic also has a limited sphere of application. One of these limitations was encountered when *love* was defined. A person might reasonably argue that the definition being used for love is not logical because it assumes too much, i.e., that love is real. Love implies a selfless quality while at the same time assuming that it is the self that desires to love. Is it really possible for a self to be selfless? If I say that I want to love selflessly, isn't that a selfish desire? Such questions point to the limitations of logic.

Definitions and concepts can be logical, illogical, or alogical—outside the bounds of logic. Love, as it has been defined, is alogical. But this is not a problem. We do not need to have a logical definition of love in order to know that our love for others is real or to find satisfaction in the experience of being loved. Though logic cannot even make sense of love, *experience* can make it very real indeed.

Logic, intuition, and experience all serve important functions in the development of insight. Experience is a master teacher. Logic is a wonderfully socializable tool. Intuition is a valuable personal resource. When addressing issues that are alogical in nature (such as defining *love*) experience can atone for the limitations of logic. By respecting when situations call for logic, intuition, and experience, we access our highest wisdom in reaching decisions about what to do and what to believe.

FREEWILL

Freewill is like money. Generally, the concern is not with whether we have any, but with *how much* of it we possess. The assumption here is that when spiritual beliefs and attitude are at issue, we are rich with freewill. For countless generations, across all cultures, from all different walks of life, and with the broadest range of personal experiences, people have chosen to have faith in God. This is not an adequate reason to have faith in God. But what this does indicate is that we are very free as human beings to make choices about spiritual beliefs. Our attitude toward life is another area where we enjoy a great degree of freedom. The question, "Is the glass half empty or half full?" stands as a call to own our attitude. Belief in freewill activates the self-assertion of personal responsibility for one's attitude and spiritual beliefs. By so doing, belief in freewill makes love and faith a *real possibility.*

The importance of nature and nurture, of course, must not be ignored. The impact that these factors can have on our decision-making process spans the range from negligible to extreme. Culturally, we make allowance for extreme conditions of nature and nurture. In spiritual contexts this is expressed in terms of whether someone has been "brain washed." The domination of circumstances beyond our control is also respected in the context of our legal system. Limitations on freewill are reflected in the insanity defense and in laws that require a requisite mental capacity in order for a crime to be successfully prosecuted.

Mental retardation, extreme duress, and other circumstances can liberate us from the imposition of legal consequences for our actions. But even though the existence of extreme situations calls attention to the difficulty of defining just how free freewill is, *exceptions should not be allowed to define the rule.* The issue is not whether nature and nurture play key roles in life. The issue is the degree to which we transcend such origins with the personal empowerment and self-assertion that has come to be known as the trademark of the human spirit.

We cannot always control how full our glass is, but we can control how much we appreciate the water that is in the glass. We did not create our bodies, but how we treat them reflects our appreciation for these tabernacles of life. We cannot always control what thoughts pop into our head, but we can direct the course of our contemplation. We cannot control what our parents taught us about spirituality, but we can savor the opportunity to take personal responsibility for such matters.

We can act courageously in extremely stressful situations and take responsibility for our actions rather than make excuses. We can let go of emotional baggage. We can claim authority over our spiritual prerogatives and, by so doing, experience the reality of our freewill.

We are so free spiritually that we can even deny the existence of freewill. Freewill is similar to love in the sense that its existence can be the subject of unresolvable rhetorical debate. But it is also similar to love in that personal experience can provide a sufficiently satisfying validation of its reality. As with love, freewill is another instance where experience can compensate for the limitations of logic.

GOD

✦ ✦ ✦

Somewhere in the dictionary
There needs to be a word
To explain the unexplainable
In a way that's not absurd

We should name our greatest hope
Although we cannot prove it true
So many words to choose from
But "God" will have to do

✦ ✦ ✦

God (god), n., 1: the one Supreme Being, the creator and ruler of the universe.

This generic, dictionary definition of God works just fine. We are exploring whether generic love leads to generic faith in a generic God. There is no need for fancy packaging. This definition comes with all the nutritional value found in other, more expensive Gods. But let's read into the label just a little more to get an appreciation for the ingredients.

Supreme. In order to be supreme, God must not be found lacking in goodness, knowledge, or power. Therefore, God must be omnibenevolent, omniscient, and omnipotent. God also must not be limited in terms of space, time, or quality. So, the attributes of being infinite, eternal, and perfect are part of supremacy, as well.

Being. In this context two attributes of *being* must be recognized: freewill and personhood. Because the possibility of love is predicated on freewill and God is being defined as omnibenevolent, the freewill quality of *being* is consistent with and implicit in what has already been stated. God is also a personal being. Not a machine. Not simply a force or energy. God is a personal being who can love and be loved.

Creator. As the creator, God is our spiritual parent. Che is the source of life.

Ruler. The important connotation of this attribute is the implication that God chooses to continue being involved in our lives. Given God's goodness, this must be understood as a loving relationship.

Defining God does not make God exist, of course. Nor does it dismiss important issues such as proof of God's existence or the presence of evil. Although such concerns encourage calling into question the existence of God, they must not be allowed to define God out of existence from the start. Whether or not the state of this world is logically consistent with the existence of God will be taken up in Part III. Part II will address issues of faith—the willingness to act on belief. What needs to be tied together first is the relationship between the four pillars of perspective that have been set into place so far. These pillars are love, logic, freewill, and God. Their interrelationship, which is developed in the next chapter, will be referred to as the *Freewill Love Factor*.

HOW TO SAFELY MIX LOVE, LOGIC, FREEWILL, AND GOD

✦ ✦ ✦

Question:
>   How can you safely transport a lion
>   and a lamb in the same cage?
Answer:
>   Make two trips.

✦ ✦ ✦

When Selfish Sam drove to work each day, he would pass by the bus stop a block from his house. Long-Sufferin' Luke was always standing there in the weather, waiting by the curb. Because Sam and Luke happened to work in the same office building, they also often saw each other at the end of the day. Luke would see Sam walking toward the parking garage, and Sam would watch Luke running to catch the 5:10 bus. Sam never gave a thought to offering Luke a ride.

Selfish Sam lived in Buffalo, New York. People used to say he was "more foul than the weather." But Sam took little notice of the weather or what others thought of him, locked away as he was behind the tinted windows of his climate control world. There in his little sanctuary of self-absorption, Sam enjoyed every creature comfort that ever came out of Detroit. He had a control knob that could do just about everything, except make the morning coffee and provide companionship for a lonely heart.

One Sunday afternoon, Sam was hiking alone in the mountains. He, of course, had no friends with whom to share the day. And because he was alone, he had plenty of time to think about how important it was to him to be selfish. He believed that everyone was just as selfish as he was, the only difference was that they tried to hide it in order to get what they wanted. This perspective led Sam to hate deception above all other offenses to ethics and morality. For although Sam was selfish, his ego nonetheless found great comfort in thinking that it owned the moral high ground.

As Sam walked along his chosen path, he reflected on the value of his selfish perspective on life. Suddenly, for no apparent reason, the air became very still around him and the sounds of nature ceased. Sam watched in amazement as the clouds in front of him began to part. As they did, a soft, shimmering, golden light poured down from the heavens. Then, the voice of God spoke to him saying, "I am your God, Sam. All people on this earth are my children. I love you all and want you to love each other. Now, go and act accordingly!"

Selfish Sam was awe-struck. But awe was not all that he felt. This unexpected appearance of God was also an annoying source of cognitive dissonance. The last thing Sam wanted was a paradigm shift, and no god was about to spoil his attempts to commune with nature. Once he regained his composure, the mental tools he had purchased with a lifetime of persistent skepticism were again at his disposal.

"How do I know that you really are God and that I am not just dreaming this?" he demanded.

Then God, who is always so cool, answered, "Tell me what it takes to convince you, Sam, and I will prove it to your satisfaction."

So Sam asked for his proof and God gave it to him.[2]

Then God said, "Now that you know I exist and that I want you to act with love (as that term was defined in chapter one of Halbert Katzen's *The Logic of Love*), I expect I can rely on your whole-hearted cooperation."

"God knows, you will certainly get my cooperation," responded Selfish Sam. "I know how to apply standards as well as anyone. You can rely on me for that much. But I'm not sure what you mean by "whole-hearted." As I understand Halbert's use of the term love, it stands for a freewill interplay between attitude and action. If the actions of love are *required*, this pulls the plug on the current of freewill. The *experience* of the reality of one's love is lost once the acts of love become coerced. Perhaps, God, you should reread his chapter on freewill if you are still unclear about this.

---

[2]For maximum impact, assume that the proof Selfish Sam wanted was exactly the same one that you would want.

"I must admit, this revelation of yourself is an extraordinary event that will change my life forever. It makes the personal value of acting with love a lot less glorious, however, because I feel far less free to act than when I woke up this morning. If acting with love was against the law, I could certainly get out of it by claiming extreme duress. After all, I understand your willingness to extend mercy is balanced by ultimate justice. Fair as you may be in your perfect administration of these values, my freewill is very sensitive to the significance of anticipated outcomes. The last thing I want to do is open myself up to your judgment by acting out in unloving ways.

"And while we're on the subject of love, seeing you here in all your power and glory, I cannot begin to understand why you would fill a whole planet with such a selfish and deceitful lot. I cannot imagine growing to love them. After all, aren't we humans in the habit of killing the best and brightest promoters of love? Nevertheless, I know what it means to act in the interests of others and will go forth to do so. Who am I to deny God?"

On his way to work the next day, Selfish Sam spotted Long-Sufferin' Luke at the bus stop. Without hesitation, Sam pulled up to the bus stop. He offered Luke a ride, confident that he was acting in accordance with God's will. Luke didn't even have time to put on his seatbelt before Sam started talking a mile a minute about how his life had changed since he met God.

"Of course, I do not expect that you are any more loveable than...well, than me, for instance," explained Sam. "But hey, if God says I should do good acts for others, so be it. I tried to tell chen that I think we're all just a bunch of jerks, anyway. So what's the point, right? But che's on a heavy benevolence trip, so I said I'd play along!"

What Sam did not realize was that Luke had been harboring deep resentments toward Sam for years. It started one foul day several winters back when Sam soaked Luke with slush while driving past him at the bus stop. Luke had always been able to sense that Sam was thoroughly selfish. And that slush was the last straw. Luke swore on that day that if Sam ever gave him cause for offense again, he would shoot Sam three times in the heart. So ever since then, Luke carried around a .357 Magnum, just in case cause was given.

Well, nothing offended Luke more than when people pretend to care because they have to, rather than because they want to. So, when he heard how Sam was only being nice because God said he had to be, Long-Sufferin' Luke pulled out his .357 Magnum and shot Selfish Sam three times in the heart. As Luke put his gun back in its holster, he smiled as he considered that he really had done Sam a favor. He figured that Sam would have suffered more had he lived out the rest of his life from a place that left his freewill with no meaningful choice.

The story of Selfish Sam reveals the nature of what I call life's *Freewill Love Factor*. The Freewill Love Factor stands for the appreciation of how a revelation of God can undermine our opportunity to know that our love is real, that it is not coerced by a fear of ultimate judgment. Love, as an attitude put into action, cannot be coerced. Coercion makes it extremely difficult to assess motivation. It undermines our ability to experience service to others as the reflection of a loving attitude. Love and selfishness may at times motivate the same actions, but they never produce the same inner experience.

Wake-up calls are a double-edged sword. Though they may motivate us to do what is right, overwhelming experiences can galvanize fear-based motivations as powerfully as they can inspire an attitude of love. The one thing that Sam and Luke had in common was that they both hated what Sam had become—a slave to the fear of judgment. A world where Selfish Sam can exist is a world that maximizes the experience of freewill, and this, in turn, is what makes the attitude of love so beautiful and good. The perception of the possibility that our actions may not have consequences, that there is no ultimate form of justice, gives freewill a field to play on and provides the best experiential assurance that love is real.

The Freewill Love Factor not only holds open the possibility of experiencing the reality of our love for others, but also enables us to experience receiving love from others. The temptation is always present to question someone's sincerity when they are pressured to act in a certain way. Remember when you were young and some kid did something mean to you? And then chens mother made chen apologize. Remember how hollow the words "I'm sorry." sounded?

It may be okay for biological parents to require their children to exhibit social grace. But the Freewill Love Factor reflects how things need to work out differently on the spiritual level. Spiritual freedom is crucial. That we can only approach God through faith assures that we do not miss out on the thrilling opportunity to experience the reality of love.

Many people claim to have direct experience with God. Whether it's feeling the presence of God, being miraculously healed, raising the dead, or parting the sea, people have long asserted that the reality of God can be experienced. Is this inconsistent with what has just been stated about the relationship between love and freewill? Not at all. On the contrary, for those who have faith in God, the progressive development of love-motivated acts increasingly safeguards freewill from being overawed by experiences of God. If we *first* demonstrate our love through the choices we make in life, *then* our willingness to do this before ever having a knowledge of God can work to safeguard our appreciation for the reality of love.

There are countless opportunities every day—some big, some small—to love. If we are willing to love first, then the progressive accumulation of these experiences make it possible to progressively experience God without endangering the opportunity to appreciate the experience of love. At least in theory, a love-motivated life should have the potential to make what would be impossible (freewill and the experience of God) possible.

The refusal to have faith in God guarantees that no experience in life can be interpreted as an experience of God. The necessity of believing in God in advance of experiencing God is a reasonable and wise door of separation because this preserves the integrity of love and freewill. The willingness to hold love as the highest value is the key to this door. Such a supreme assertion of human thought—to believe and act for the sake of love—is the essence of faith.

If love is the supreme value, and if we are to know by our experience that love is real in our lives, then experiences with God must be in proportion to the quality of faith-activated love that we demonstrate in our lives. This is not to say that we must have faith in God in order to know that love is real. This is only to say that we cannot know that our love is real if we first have knowledge of God's existence. For this reason, faith in God—the willingness to act upon belief—is a plausible way to transcend the limitations of the Freewill Love Factor without sacrificing freewill.

PART 2

FAITH

With an understanding of the Freewill Love Factor under our belts, we can now explore the special nature of spiritual faith. The material in Part II sorts through the differences between belief and knowledge as these terms are applied in a spiritual versus a secular context. It focuses on the implications of making a decision that is intended to be a life-long reaffirmation of belief. Additionally, Part II considers the propriety, when considering faith in God, of accepting the testimony of others (in contrast with relying on one's own thoughts and experiences). The last chapter is addressed to those who already have faith. It highlights the importance of progressively developing a love-motivated faith and speaks to the value of experiencing faith as a logical extension of love.

A DEFINITION BEYOND WORDS

✦ ✦ ✦

The Gravity Song

When I was back in college, I wanted for to know
All about the gravity and just what makes it go
So, I signed up for the science class, sat myself down
I asked the professor, "Hey, what keeps us on the ground?"
    He said, "That's easy, boy. What it is, is the gravity."
    And I said, "What's that?"
    And he said, "That is what keeps us on the ground!" . . .

Now the physics professor, he met me with a laugh
I asked him about gravity and he drew me up a graph
He punched a bunch of numbers on a little calculator
And said, "The object with lesser mass is attracted to the greater!"
    I said, "Thanks. I can see that. I was wondering why."
    He says, "Well, it's gravity!"

Well, I talked to them professors. I learned a lot of things
About the rate of falling objects and the way a pendulum swings
They can calculate it, corner it, predict it like a wiz
And there isn't one among 'em that can tell you what it is
    Of course, I can tell you what it is . . .
    Gravity is all them folks believing in it
                keeping you on the ground!

Steve Clark

Trying to define the essence of faith in God is like trying to explain what makes gravity exist. Pushing on the scientific mystery of gravity helps define the difference between philosophy and science. Notwithstanding that philosophy and science are interrelated, they are two different conversations. Talking about the mystery of gravity, however intellectually stimulating that may be, will not help us discover that objects fall at thirty-two feet per second squared. Similarly, pushing on the spiritual mystery of faith helps us respect the difference between offering inspiration and communicating content. Communication designed for inspiration produces deep feelings. Such forms of expression have their own value, but they can cloud the reasoning abilities of the mind. An exploration of the logic of love is an adventure into the highest realms of thought and requires dispassionate analysis.

Gravity is a mystery because we cannot find cause for its existence. Faith is a mystery because human beings are all over the board on this subject. There will always be a mysterious aspect to faith due to its intimate association with freewill and love. We must keep in mind that we are traveling in the realm of the alogical. On a certain level, the answer to "Why have faith in God?" has already been given. The answer is love. But this *explains* nothing. There is value in knowing how gravity works, even though the source of this energy is beyond explanation. Similarly, there is value in understanding how faith works, even though the alogical definitions of love and freewill mean we'll never be able to *prove* anything.

Like gravity, faith has observable qualities and, to a certain extent, acts in ways that are predictable. As a practical matter, understanding how faith operates and using it effectively is similar to observing how gravity works and applying that understanding wisely. Sometimes all we really need to do is "calculate it, corner it, and predict it like a wiz." Discerning how faith works is critical for determining whether it best fosters love. Fortunately, as with gravity, when it comes to the issue of application, there is a lot about faith that is not shrouded in mystery. We do not need to penetrate the mysteries of natural forces to roll down a hill. Nor do we need to penetrate the mysteries of faith in order to appreciate the benefit of raising a sail to its favorable winds.

THE DANGER OF FAITH BASED ON ANECDOTES

✦ ✦ ✦

One day Diane asked her mother, "When you prepare roast beef for baking, why do you always cut the ends off of it?"

"Well, that's how your grandmother taught me to do it. And since hers came out perfect every time, I have always followed her instructions to the letter," Diane's mother explained.

Diane went to her grandmother and asked her why she always cut off the ends of the roast beef. Her grandmother responded, "I learned how to make it from your great grandmother, Diane. She taught me when I was just a little girl. People didn't go to restaurants very often, back then. That's why daughters took great pride in learning how to cook from their mothers. It was a very special mother-daughter thing to do back then."

Fortunately, Diane's great grandmother was still alive. So, she called her great grandmother to ask the reason for cutting off the ends of the roast beef. Her great grandmother answered, "Well, in my day ovens were not nearly so big as what you

> have today. I had to cut the ends off so that it
> would fit. Why do you ask, dear? Is there
> something wrong?"

✦ ✦ ✦

When I was in college, my friend Danny had a terrible car accident. A drunk driver entered the highway from an exit ramp and plowed into him head on. Fortunately, Danny was wearing his seat belt; it saved his life. Though he has recovered very well from the accident, he did sustain serious injuries. You can be spared the details of those injuries, but he could not be. When I saw him in the intensive care unit shortly after the accident, the reality of it all hit me hard, and it hurt me. Through the suffering that I experienced with Danny, I learned a few things.

First, I learned to wear my seatbelt. (I knew to not drink and drive. Otherwise, that would have been the first lesson.)

Second, I learned that I was the kind of person who had to have one of my dearest friends almost killed in a car accident before I would learn to wear my seatbelt. This scared me. It scared me because I knew that I had already had plenty of life experience to bring me to the decision to wear a seatbelt. I realized that I had been slow in learning to see to my own safety. The acceptance of this self-administered critique led to an appreciation of the danger of using anecdotal experience for reaching general conclusions.

In this particular instance the anecdote leads to what I still believe is a good habit. But, the emotional impact of Danny's accident also reminded me that, even though emotions may at times be a catalyst for making a good choice, they can also cloud judgment. Powerful anecdotes make it all too easy to overinflate the importance of a specific outcome. What if Danny had died with his seatbelt on? Would that experience have caused me to undervalue the use of seatbelts?

What if I made this whole thing up? What if I didn't? Why should it matter whether the story is true? *Knowing* what actually happened to Danny is not nearly so important as *understanding* what could happen to any of us. Sometimes the important information for making a decision is an awareness of the possibilities and probabilities. The decision to wear a seatbelt should be based on what can generally happen to us in cars, not on what specifically happened to Danny.

Danny's story is a good story for promoting the importance of wearing seatbelts. It happens to be true. However, when it comes to making decisions that are regularly reaffirmed, it is better that we should get the lesson from the more stable foundation of reason. The fickle foundation of anecdote-related emotion can lead to making unwise decisions. I do not mean to discount the value of personal experience. Rather, I wish to emphasize that the use of reason serves us well in reaching decisions that are regularly reaffirmed. By using reason, rather than waiting for experience, we can more quickly enjoy the benefits of embracing good lifestyle choices. Additionally, this approach offers wisdom that can be shared with others more easily because it generalizes, rather than individualizes, experience.

There is no place this principle can be better applied than to the decision that is the primary subject of this book—whether to have faith in God. This is not to suggest that we should be unemotional about the topic of faith, but the decision to have faith in God should not be based on emotion. Faith in God is not something to be fickle about. When chosen, faith is supposed to enjoy a lifetime of reaffirmation. The best hope for a lifetime of faith is to build it on the more solid foundation of reason and life's most universal experiences.

The use of anecdotal experiences for promoting faith in God is a little bit more complicated than an issue like wearing seatbelts. If Danny were ever to say, "Trust me. Seatbelts save lives. I know because a seatbelt saved my life," a reasonable response would be, "It is not that I don't trust you, but this is an issue where we can get statistical information relevant to making a reasoned decision. Even though what you say makes sense, a better source of information for reaching this decision is the available statistics. Therefore, trusting you should not even be an issue. There may be other areas of life where trusting you would be appropriate. This just doesn't happen to be one of them."

A conversation about having faith in God goes down a little differently because we cannot turn to statistics. Instead of statistics, the appropriate resource is one's own inner experience. If I say to someone who does not have faith, "Trust me. God saves lives. I know because God saved my life," a reasonable response would be, "It is not that I don't trust you, but trusting your experience as the basis for my sense of reality is not appropriate. This is even recognized by most of the world's religions inasmuch as they celebrate rituals marking a child's entrance into spiritual adulthood around puberty. The acceptance of personal responsibility for one's faith reflects mature self-empowerment. If I choose faith, it should be an expression of me, of who I am. There may be other areas of life where trusting you would be appropriate. This just doesn't happen to be one of them."

Giving testimonials has proven to be an effective way of winning converts, especially when the testimonial involves an extraordinary event or a claim that a miracle occurred. But the use of such tactics can lead people to think of faith in God as something that is situation-specific. I do not wish to take a position on the truth of all the testimonials offered by people over the course of human history. But trying to convince people that they should have faith in God because they should trust the truth of someone's story is not the best approach. It can lead to two mistaken conclusions. The first is that there is no better reason to give for having faith in God. The second is that God's grace is random or, even worse, that God plays favorites.

Faith in God need not be based on anecdotal experiences. When faith is based on a unique experience, it fails to offer a good example of a path that is equally accessible to all. In contrast to this, when the basis for faith is a commitment to love as the highest value, then faith rests on the bedrock of an enduring spiritual value with universal appeal. If faith can be seen as a reasonable extension of love, then there is no need to look for a better reason.

THE KNOWLEDGE-VERSUS-BELIEF DILEMMA

✦ ✦ ✦

Things are known in the knower after the manner of the knower,
not after their own manner of existence.
Thomas Aquinas

✦ ✦ ✦

We go on quests for knowledge, not for belief.
Knowledge is worthy of a quest because we value taking
actions that are in harmony with this thing called "reality."
Knowledge reflects a clear perception of reality; belief implies
the possibility of error. When something passes for
knowledge, this means that people share a common view of
reality on that issue. But the line between knowledge and
belief is hard to define because our experience and our
thoughts about life are subjective and individual in nature.
This prevents the claim of knowledge from being absolute.
At best, we *believe* that we possess knowledge.

"How do you *know* that San Francisco
really exists," asks the Eternal Skeptic?
"Well, I've commuted there each day for

the past ten years. Why? What's your point?" responds the bewildered Realist.

"How do you know you didn't dream it? How do you know you are not dreaming right now? Maybe you're just a brain in a jar with electrodes that stimulate you into thinking these experiences are real," muses the Eternal Skeptic. "You can't prove otherwise! You can't really *know* anything."

"I know God exists from my experience with chen," chimes in the Faithful One.

"But you don't *really* know," barks back the Eternal Skeptic. "No one can really know anything!"

Then, employing the Eternal Skeptic's own premise, the Faithful One retorts, "Then you cannot know that I do not know because your own experience and reasoning discredits any claim of knowledge. Therefore, the possibility of knowing God through faith is still an open question. Besides, at least the knowledge I claim is based on experience with God. If the validation of knowledge is possible, there can be no better validation than experience with God."

"I'm grateful for how the Faithful One seems to have saved me from the Eternal Skeptic's existential, epistemological entrapments," interrupts the Realist. "But I have a real job and mouths to feed at home. I presume none of these cosmic insights will keep me from dinner tonight or work tomorrow. That being the case, I'm out of here. You two can banter back and forth 'til the break of day, for all I care."

"I will not be adding anything that would keep you from work and family," responds the

Faithful One. "However, I do hope to offer
some thoughts that might greatly enhance your
experience of work and your love for your
family."

The Eternal Skeptic has a lot more to offer the discussion
than the suggestion that we might be nothing more than brains
in jars. The absurdity of that scenario is evidence of just how
obtuse the topic of spirituality can become. Speculating about
the nature of spiritual life opens the door on a metaphysical
three-ring circus, complete with clowns and wild animals, as
well as death-defying acts of love, loyalty, and courage. It's a
psychological thrill ride where we free-fall down the Tower of
Gloom, soil ourselves in the Haunted Mansion From Hell, and
get turned every which way but loose on life's little roller-
coaster ride of cosmological chaos. Turn your back for one
minute, and the next thing you know, Aunt Betty just spent all
her money getting financial advice from some psychic hotline.

So why believe in anything at all? Just because enough
people agree on a set of spiritual beliefs that it's called a
religion, does this make it any more probable than the "Brain-
In-A-Jar" theory of existence? The discussion between the
Realist, the Faithful One, and the Eternal Skeptic helps keep us
on track in two ways. First, by exposing the elusive nature of
knowledge (when it comes to discussions about reality), these
predisposed pundits focus us on the fuzzy boundary between
belief and knowledge. Second, they remind us that regardless
of what we believe, we still have to make choices about how to
deal with life; we still need to get to work and procreate for the
privilege of pondering these seemingly impenetrable
possibilities.

Let's enter this quagmire by generating a working
definition of knowledge. We do not need to get worked up
into existential dilemmas over defining knowledge. We just
need to get enough of a handle on this concept to get us to
the grocery store and back. Philosophic discussions about
knowledge may get obtuse, but practical use of the term enjoys

a narrower range of opinion. The standard for what *passes for knowledge* is not so elusive, though it does vary between things spiritual and things material.

Identifying the differing standards for knowledge allows us to work with the concept on a day to day basis. With material things, whether something is accepted as fact or not has a lot to do with how many people believe it. The existence of San Francisco passes for knowledge because no one cares to call it into question. On the other hand, who was involved in killing President Kennedy is still an open question. Positions taken on this subject are, therefore, relegated to the status of belief.

In the spiritual realm we do not enjoy the benefit of commonly held standards or measuring devices that yield replicable results. Consequently, the reality of anything spiritual can only be a subjective interpretation of an inner, or what might be called a *supermaterial*, reality. Because no one can hand us a prepackaged experience of God, the process whereby spiritual belief develops into knowledge does not follow the same pattern of acceptance as with material reality beliefs. Coming to a common belief in the reality of God is not like promulgating the discovery that the world is round. With things spiritual, the *quality* of personal experience is more significant than the *quantity* of people who claim to have a similar experience. Therefore, the first practical appreciation of this distinction between material knowledge and spiritual knowledge is that the source for material knowledge comes from outside ourselves, while the source for spiritual knowledge must be validated from our inner experience of life.

The second lesson arrives with the departure of the Realist. It is that no matter where we fall on this issue of knowledge and belief, ultimately we must act. Our lives are not "on hold" while we try to figure these things out. As much as we might like to act with knowledge (or something approximating knowledge), on the material level we cannot always afford to wait for that degree of certainty. And on the spiritual level, whatever degree of certainty that we enjoy is one that cannot readily be offered to others. Even if the Faithful One makes a good point about appealing to the best possible source for knowledge of reality (God), chens ability to form the sentence does not make the content real for anyone else.

Actions based upon knowledge are preferable to those based on belief because of the value of taking actions that are in harmony with reality. Actions based on belief fail to provide the sense of security that actions based on knowledge provide. For this reason when it comes to issues of spirituality, people without faith in God sometimes believe themselves to be in a superior position in refusing to believe what cannot be proven. But, as the dialogue between The Eternal Skeptic and The Faithful One demonstrates, when it comes to things spiritual, neither side is in a superior position.

Faith is what brings life to beliefs. Beliefs may be shared, facts may pass for knowledge, but faith is a purely personal experience that is evidenced through actions. Faith, whether it relates to secular or spiritual beliefs, is where the rubber meets the road. In a secular context, the distinction between belief and knowledge is predicated on consensus because this is how we arrive at secular knowledge. In a spiritual context, the distinction between belief and knowledge is a personal matter because the source for knowledge comes from within. These distinctions are foundational for appreciating the need for two different understandings of faith, one for the secular context and one for the spiritual context.

WHY SPIRITUAL BELIEFS LOOK LIKE SECULAR KNOWLEDGE

✦ ✦ ✦

Know what you believe, and believe what you know.

✦ ✦ ✦

Similar to the word *love*, the word *faith* takes on different meaning depending on the contexts in which it appears. As the willingness to act on belief, faith finds expression in both secular and spiritual life. Unlike the word *love*, however, *faith* appears in contexts that do not enjoy as much consistency of interpretation. If I say that I love ice cream, our common appreciation for food is enough to avoid confusion. No one exchanges wedding vows with their favorite flavor of ice cream. On the other hand, not everyone relates to having faith in God. In fact, those with faith in God do not always recognize a commonality of experience with each other.

Generating an appreciation for the context of spiritual faith begins with an exploration of the attitudes associated with secular knowledge and belief. This will be used to lay a foundation for understanding why spiritual beliefs get treated like secular knowledge. This chapter will conclude by creating a distinction between religious beliefs and personal faith. This provides a framework for looking at the relationship between spiritual faith and the Freewill Love Factor.

> "Why did you put water in your gas tank instead of gasoline?" asks R. U. Alrite.
> "I don't know. If it wasn't temporary insanity, then there's something else terribly wrong with me," responds I. M. Knutz.

Act against knowledge and you are on your way to the loony bin.

> "You always said that you didn't believe capital punishment was justifiable. So, why did you just vote in favor of it on the referendum?" inquiries Ima Shauct.
> "I don't know. I guess I changed my mind. But there's no denying one thing: actions speak louder than words. I guess I really do believe in capital punishment after all," explains Joy S. Freedom.

Act against belief and you simply changed your mind.

In the secular world, whatever passes for knowledge has reached a requisite level of consensus. The line that separates knowledge from belief is not an absolute, though; people do not always agree on what should pass for knowledge. But when there is agreement, then the attitudes that come into play are those associated with claims of knowledge. These attitudes must not be taken lightly; they define the boundaries between sanity and insanity. If we keep doing things like putting water in our gas tank, eventually the men in white suits show up with a straightjacket, offering a room right next to Mr. I. M. Knutz.

The foundation for this attitude regarding sanity is created by the consensus that exists not only at the level of the object of knowledge, but more importantly, at the level of what it takes to validate knowledge. It is at this deeper level that our "reality buttons" get pushed. Knowing what is real is important to us, and it should be. It is hard enough to work together when we don't agree on what is real, but when we cannot even agree on what *method* to use for deciding what is real, this can trigger major trust and intimacy issues. Although the "scientific method" may not be perfectly defined or universally agreed upon in every respect, it provides a high degree of stability in discovering what is real in secular contexts.

Questions of secular knowledge do not inquire into *who* we are, only *what* we are or what something else is. For this reason, issues of secular knowledge are safe for the psyche to enter. We can go marching bravely into the secular world of discovery, psychologically protected in the armor of social acceptance. The quest for secular knowledge does not threaten our sense of self, and it is a quest that can be directly shared with others. Consequently, one of the benefits of the quest for secular knowledge is that there is no shame in being wrong.

If, for instance, we want to know whether Mt. Everest really is the highest mountain, we can gather up our best instruments and go measure it against the other contenders. If our measurements say that it is, then this is easily accepted as knowledge. If better instruments later reveal that a different mountain is higher, no one is labeled a lunatic for having previously claimed to *know* that Mt. Everest was the highest mountain. In fact, what passes for knowledge on this subject could go back and forth several times during the course of investigation. If investigation repeatedly yields different results, then the worth of the measuring instruments may be called into question, but the methodology for acquiring knowledge will not be.

When it comes to the issue of sanity, secular beliefs

receive completely different treatment than does secular knowledge. The realm of belief is marked by tolerance, by an appreciation that reasonable minds may differ. This liberal attitude diminishes only at the extreme ends of the spectrum—when there seems to be no basis for the belief or when consensus is being approached. As evidence accumulates and a pool of experience develops around a certain subject, we think differently about unpopular positions. We begin applying the attitude associated with secular knowledge: that contrary positions are crazy.

In general, in the realm of belief, we are not disparaged for making use of anecdotal experience, having personal preferences, or offering subjective interpretations. Beliefs enjoy a far more liberal standard for acceptance than do claims of knowledge. This liberal standard is what creates the need for the word *faith*. Faith stands for the willingness to act upon belief. The difference between faith and "blind faith" is the degree to which our willingness to act on belief is supported by previous experience and logic.

If Faith, the mother of Hope, has picked up Hope after school for the last three months without incident, then her previous experience justifies her faith that Hope will be there when she goes to pick her up today. If an accident has landed Hope in the hospital, then Faith's hope would be dashed to pieces. But Faith's faith—her activated belief— would be no less wise. Faith's faith that Hope is waiting for her is justified because anomalous occurrences do not detract from the wisdom of secular faith. Therefore, Faith is not blind in her expectation that Hope will be waiting for her. (Fortunately, these morbid speculations about Hope being hurt never happened. Faith and Hope will be reunited today, just as they always have been.)

This understanding of faith is adequate for secular activities. In a spiritual context, however, faith takes on new dimensions of meaning and value because it is used not only to motivate our actions, but also to define who we are and the nature of our relationship to others.

Secular knowledge is largely a matter of consensus, whereas spiritual knowledge is a purely personal experience. In contrast with secular contexts, the transition from spiritual belief to spiritual knowledge is not a matter of more people supporting a given belief. Because the transition from spiritual belief to spiritual knowledge is self-defined, and because faith in God is supposed to be a lifelong decision, the attitudes associated with spiritual beliefs are generally similar to those associated with secular knowledge.

Let's say Mr. M. I. Shore decides to have faith in God. Then, a decade or so later, he rejects his faith. He will tend to look back on his faith as though he had been acting against knowledge. At best, he will think that stress caused him to need a crutch. At worst, he will think he must have been self-deluded, crazy. This type of hindsight occurs because spiritual faith is supposed to open the door to an experience of God—the supreme architect of reality. Even if Mr. M. I. Shore never claimed to really "know" God exists, because spiritual faith is supposed to be whole-hearted and life-long, spiritual belief effects the psyche in a way similar to secular knowledge.

Generally, the experience of changing *faith-beliefs* is very stressful. Faith-beliefs are those beliefs that are a fundamental part of one's spiritual faith; they are the beliefs that define who we are and what our relationship is to others. Sometimes they take the form of personal affirmations such as "I am a child of God." When religions specify faith-beliefs, they are sometimes referred to as essential doctrines or creeds. Examples include, "Hear, oh Israel, the Lord our God the Lord is One," "The Bible is the Word of God," and "There is no God but Allah, and Mohammed is his prophet."

Faith-beliefs do not enjoy the liberal tolerance for change that are accorded secular beliefs. The secular world can withstand changes in what passes for knowledge because the methodology is not being brought into question. In contrast, changes in faith-beliefs call into question the quality of the methodology that was initially used in formulating them.

This is destabilizing on a psychological level because the methodology for developing faith-beliefs is so extremely personal.

Although the world of secular discovery enjoys the benefit of a relaxed attitude toward changes in belief, this comes at the price of having to rely on others for what passes for knowledge, for what is secularly real. In the realm of spiritual life changes in faith-beliefs are psychologically disconcerting, but this realm also offers the hope of supreme knowledge—spiritual knowledge based on experience with God. The secular world offers safety in numbers because agreement determines what is secularly real. In contrast, the spiritual realm offers the freedom of self-empowerment for the purpose of determining what is spiritually real.

Relating to spiritual beliefs in a way that is similar to secular knowledge does not necessarily create problems on a personal level. Treating spiritual beliefs in a similar fashion as secular knowledge reflects a natural outgrowth of taking personal responsibility for one's whole-hearted decisions about spiritual life. This is consistent with the dynamic of the Freewill Love Factor because the personal experience of spiritual beliefs operates in a similar way to believing that our love is real and that we enjoy freewill. Faith, love, and freewill are all unprovable self-assertions about what is real.

No one else can prove to us that our love is real. The secular world of discovery cannot help us answer such a personal question. Those around us may offer comfort, but we can only look within ourselves for confirmation. Because of the personal challenge associated with taking complete responsibility for our faith-beliefs, and because of the consensus comfort associated with the acceptance of secular knowledge, there is a temptation to turn to religion as a source for faith-beliefs in order to enjoy the security of group association. This shifts the responsibility for spiritual knowledge away from the individual and onto the group. It obscures the distinction between the social qualities of religious experience and inner qualities of individual spiritual experience.

When *religious belief* is not sufficiently differentiated from *spiritual faith*, then spiritual experience stands in danger of losing its self-authenticating nature. This is the difference between bringing spirituality to the practice of religion and looking to religion for what can only come from within. Faith is always personal. It cannot be possessed by a group. The failure to appreciate this aspect of spiritual faith is what fuels the fire of religious conflict. Spiritual knowledge can never be established by consensus.

Religions are a poor crutch for trying to bring the comforts of consensus to personal spiritual experience. This is not to downplay the enriching experiences that religion—the socialization of spiritual experience—can provide. Trying to find God through religion, however, is very different from finding God personally and then bringing that relationship to one's religious experiences. Choosing to go where the supreme value of love leads is a personal journey. Exploring faith in God as a possible way to best live the value of love requires that we remain personally empowered when deciding which beliefs should attain the status of faith-beliefs. To do this, we need to have an understanding of spiritual faith that embraces a quest for spiritual knowledge through personal spiritual experience.

FAITH TO LAST A LIFETIME

◆ ◆ ◆

The last step depends on the first.
The first step depends on the last.
Rene Daumall

◆ ◆ ◆

Spiritual faith must not be taken lightly. It takes on the emotional attitudes associated with secular knowledge, but without providing the stability of a shared methodology for discovery. On the other hand, there is nothing wrong with being light-hearted. The decision to have faith in God need not drive us crazy. Though spiritual faith is a purely personal decision, it is a mountain that most people climb. Even if we must each blaze our own trail up this mountain, we all have what it takes to get there. All kinds of people have faith in God.

The question of whether or not to have faith in God is not one where we should defer to some supposed expert. No one else's credentials are superior to our own on this issue. We cannot hope to find outside ourselves what can only be found within. But with this personal power comes personal responsibility. Taking responsibility for the method by which we approach the issue of faith is essential for making a decision intended for lifelong re-affirmation.

The methodology being promoted here is the logic of love. The commitment to the value of love is essential. Holding love as the highest value provides stability for faith by securely anchoring our intentions in the depth of our hearts. The hope for experiencing the validation of faith is in the process of continually re-affirming whole-hearted faith.

Even though children may develop faith as a natural outgrowth of how they are raised, eventually such faith must come from a personal commitment rather than trust in one's parents. Not surprisingly, most religious traditions provide rituals for this transition around the time children reach the onset of puberty. For some of these young adults, this age may be too young for them to fully appreciate such ceremonies, and they may perform the rituals without taking them seriously. Nonetheless, these age-long traditions of the world's religions reflect the importance of taking personal responsibility for spiritual beliefs. Hopefully, by the time children have the ability to procreate, they have been taught to appreciate the value of taking responsibility for their spiritual life.

The willingness to consider having faith in God implies that one has had sufficient experience and has developed sufficient wisdom to make such a choice. The corollary to this is that no new experience or wisdom can reverse the decision to have faith. Whether such a position is closed-minded and arrogant or is the act of a mature adult depends on what side of the decision one is on. This is not to say that people with faith are never closed-minded and arrogant, nor does it mean that one cannot be a mature adult without faith in God. The point is simply that the decision to have faith is a very adult decision. If we decide to have faith, then later on stop reaffirming this choice, we have perpetrated the ultimate psychological fraud upon ourselves. Regardless of how faith starts, it must grow into an increasingly mature and self-aware decision if we are to have any hope that its fruits will ripen into an experiential knowledge of God.

FEELING FAITHFUL VERSUS CHOOSING FAITH

✦ ✦ ✦

The weak indulge in resolutions, but the strong act.
Life is but a day's work—do it well.
The Urantia Book, p. 556

✦ ✦ ✦

Faith as a feeling and faith as a choice are two entirely separate entities. Feelings may or may not come as a response to that thing called reality. When we watch a movie, for example, we suspend disbelief and emotionally live in the story. We can have deep feelings about it, even though we understand that what we're responding to is not real. This is in contrast to faith, where we are acting on beliefs which we relate to as reflections of reality.

Sometimes our emotions are a combination of reality and self-created fiction. For instance, many of us have made and broken the traditional New Year's resolution. We nurtured the resolution during December. We visualized how our lives could be better and how we would make it happen. With a couple drinks in us at the New Year's party, our resolve blossomed into vivid visions of personal transformation and renewal.

Perhaps the resolution was to exercise regularly, and the

endorphins produced from jogging provided us a nice "runner's high" during the month of January. There was some reality to the resolution. But then, February came—a sobering month—and rationalization became the new drug of choice. The commitment we once had to exercise four days a week got replaced by the excuse that a few extra pounds during the winter helps keep a body warm.

Then, we wonder: how is it that the feeling was so strong, so real, so compelling, yet the follow through is so lame, so self-defeating, so embarrassing? So when the holiday season comes the following year, we keep our mouths shut. Our friends start spouting off their inspired New Year's resolutions, and we just smile and say, "Go for it, baby!" But inside we feel the conflict of two competing, yet equally deplorable, attitudes: "They'll eat their words," and "If they stick with it, there must be something wrong with me."

What are the underlying issues that keep us from following through with our commitment to be the best we can be? It's a good question to ponder, however, it is beyond the scope of this discussion. The point here is that, if there is a God, che is all too aware of the difference between our resolutions and our follow through. If we expect to experience a miracle simply because we feel so strongly or pray so hard, because we hurt so much or feel so connected, then all we have really done is create an excuse for giving up on faith. If we are to have faith, then it must come with the trust that God is not hiding, but rather taking cognizance of the depth of our faith and respecting the Freewill Love Factor.

If we try to measure our faith by the depth of our emotions, we are headed for trouble. Emotions ebb and flow even when the facts remain the same. When we visit a friend in the hospital after an accident, we can be crying one minute and laughing the next. The emotional tide related to faith in God flows back and forth just the same. However, when the *choice* to be faithful becomes a supreme assertion of thought because it is seen as the most reasonable approach to living our most cherished value (love), we have adopted a stabilizing methodology for approaching the decision to be faithful.

A FEW WORDS TO THE FAITHFUL

✦ ✦ ✦

Those heading in the same direction
have no need to cross paths.

✦ ✦ ✦

Developing an understanding of how faith in God is a
logical extension of love provides a valuable spiritual
resource for those who already have faith. It can be of benefit
in three ways. First, inasmuch as we are all imperfect, our
faith is motivated by a combination of love and selfishness.
In order for our spiritual lives to progress, we must be
vigilant in nurturing our selfless motivations. An intellectual
appreciation of faith as an extension of love helps reinforce
this connection. Second, because logical reasoning can be
shared with others, faith held as a logical extension of love
becomes a philosophically defensible position. It can also be
offered to others for their consideration. Third, by appealing
to love as the reason for faith and boiling down the essence of
faith in God to its barest essentials, we create an opportunity
to be progressively, spiritually unified. We are less likely to
feel divided by theological doctrines and ecclesiastical
authorities when we approach faith as an outgrowth of love.

For the Love of Love

Faith is motivated by the desire to selflessly serve and by the selfish desire for salvation. The distinction, however, between love-motivated faith and selfishly motivated faith is not an either/or thing. As imperfect beings, our faith is a mixture of motivations. The question is not whether our faith is black or white, selfless or selfish, but what shade of gray, and even more importantly, whether our particular shade of gray is getting darker or lighter. Though imperfect, we still have the ability to improve, to move toward perfection. Each new day provides a new opportunity to nurture faith as a love-motivated response to life.

The selfish motivation for faith can come from a variety of places. For example, fear of death, fear of eternal damnation, the desire for salvation, or the fear of being shunned can result in the perpetuation of selfish motivations for faith. Sometimes the anxiety of a personal crisis can push us toward faith. Even a miracle of healing can produce a fear-based faith if the awe of the power to heal overshadows gratitude for the willingness to heal. (This is not a comment on whether or why God heals. The issue is that if someone believes that they have been healed, then their response can go in either or both directions — awe and gratitude.) It is my hope that by focusing on how this world can be appreciated as the creation of a loving God, and why faith is a logical extension of love, the selfish motivations will eventually atrophy and the selfless motivations will become stronger.

Intuitive Faith versus Logical Faith

There are two common forces that foster an intuitive, rather than a logical, approach to faith. First, some spiritual leaders and religious traditions teach that approaching God through logic is not only futile but spiritually arrogant. Difficult questions are portrayed as the obstacles that must be let go of in order for faith to be whole-hearted and pure.

With this approach, giving up on logic is portrayed as a necessary part of having faith. Secondly, not everyone is inclined to sit around and philosophize if it is not necessary. We do not have to be electricians to turn on the lights. Similarly, the use and enjoyment of faith does not require an explanation, only a willing attitude.

Even though logic may not be able to justify something as subjective as love, this does not mean that logic cannot justify faith once the subjective value of love has been embraced. Logic is a talent and a blessing that can be applied to the issue of faith in God. Even though intuition as well as logic can lead to faith, logic can help us ennoble and communicate the value of this insight. Most of all, learning to apply logic to spirituality helps us provide our children with a better response to their spiritual inquiries than "just because."

Being a League Player

Although some progress has been made toward inter-religious tolerance, there is still an enormous amount of work to be done. When the status of spiritual identity is based on a particular religion rather than on our individual relationship with God, our ability to become spiritually unified is in jeopardy.

Little League was created as a place for children to play, just as religion was created as a place to pray. We were not born to serve religion any more than children were born to serve Little League. If all the houses of worship sit empty, if all the sacred texts get burned, if all the rituals are forgotten, we would be no less the children of God. When, as religionists, we look at ourselves as being in the same league, we can honorably try to create the best team and have proper respect for those playing on other teams (religions). Choosing between the various teams is beyond our scope. The focus here is on being a player in God's league.

PART III

TRANSCENDING OBSTACLES TO FAITH

The goal of Part I was to create a shared understanding of the terms love, logic, freewill, and God in order to develop an appreciation for the Freewill Love Factor. The purpose of Part II was to examine the difference between spiritual faith and secular faith and to appreciate the relationship that spiritual faith has to the belief-knowledge dynamic. Additionally, it emphasized the importance of creating a stable foundation for faith, one that is self-generated and based on the value of love. What has not yet been done, and what is essential to do in order for faith to be appreciated as a logical extension of love, is make sense of this world.

At least on the surface, our world reeks with reasons to believe there is no God. These reasons have plagued people for ages in their attempts to find meaning in life and vindication for love. The goal of Part III is to respect but also to invalidate the reasoning that suggests our state of existence is inconsistent with the concept of a loving God.

RELIGION

For the sake of the argument, let's assume that religion has been a cancer running rampant through the body of human history. Even if religion is a cancer, logic would *not* support this as a reason for choosing against having faith in God. I could go out and persecute people in your name. This would not mean you actually approved of the atrocity simply because I said you did. If we are going to consider belief in God with an open mind, we should be willing to give God the benefit of this same reasoning. Diluting the *concept* of God, based on the acts of humanity, forsakes the value of objectivity. It is the ultimate in anthropomorphism to let the history of institutionalized religion define the attributes of God. This is the type of projection that religionists get criticized for.

On the other hand, we might reasonably assert that those who claim to know someone are the ones we should appeal to for information on the character of that person. For instance, let's say Harry Tymes owns a store in a dangerous neighborhood that has been robbed twice in the last week. Right after the second robbery, before he has even had time to call the police, two thugs come in, flash guns, and inform him that they work for Big Al. Harry has heard that Big Al is the local boss of organized crime. He is aware that other shop owners pay Big Al in return for "protection." The thugs, on behalf of Big Al, offer Harry Tymes protection for ten percent of his income. Even though Harry has never seen or met Big Al, he has heard enough horror stories to decide to take the deal.

These things happen. In this case, Harry's acceptance of the deal is altogether reasonable. Unfortunately, this same type of reasoning gets inappropriately applied when talking about the attributes of God and trying to understand how God is "organized." In the "Big Al" scenario, there was no particular reason to doubt the existence of Big Al, nor were there inconsistent claims about his character. In contrast, when it comes to statements about what God wants us to do or what should be done in the name of God, there is a lot of inconsistency.

Of the qualities attributed to God, the goodness of God is one of the most unquestioned. There is not always consensus as to whether the justice of God requires one to kill the "infidel" or whether the mercy of God admonishes one to try to convert the "lost soul," but love and involvement tend to be universally attributed to God. If anything, the story of the shop owner supports acceptance of the goodness of God, just as it supports accepting that Big Al is dangerous. People may differ on whether to pay off Big Al, involve the police, or run, but these options do not bring into question Big Al's character. Similarly, the various ways that religions and theologians prioritize the values refracted from the white light of love should not become a reason to question God's love.

There is no reason to consider faith in God with a defeatist attitude about the potentials of religious institutions. The issue here, however, is only individual potentials, not collective ones. Any criticism of the way others express spirituality, individually or collectively, carries with it the possibility of a better expression. Just the possibility that there can be a personally acceptable expression of spirituality is sufficient reason to consider whether faith in God might be the best expression of love.

IS IMPERFECTION A GOOD IDEA?

✦ ✦ ✦

God created perfect children
And they partied through the night
Then it began to dawn on them
That something was too right

They had known only perfection
They were always truly blessed
But they had never known triumph
Because they never faced a test

So, God created something new
Carved with wisdom out of love
Where the point is direction, not perfection
That below might smile to above

✦ ✦ ✦

It is natural to conclude that a perfect God would create a perfect life without suffering, where all the joys of heaven are shared liberally with all. In short, we would like life to fulfill our heart's desire at every moment. Anything less and, obviously, God does not exist. Imperfection seems to contradict God's benevolent omnipotence.

Heaven from birth may exist for some of God's children. Who *knows*? But what would really be so superior about an environment where no one ever exhibited glorious character traits such as altruism, loyalty, and courage? It may be a good mental exercise to contemplate how the irresistible force might move the immovable object, but good answers don't come from bad questions. Similarly, contemplating how the omnipotent God should be able to do the impossible leads nowhere. We cannot expect beautiful character traits such as altruism, loyalty, and courage to find expression where everybody and everything is (and always has been) perfect.

We don't find altruism when everything is fair and all needs are being met. Loyalty is not deeply touching when it is not tested, when there is no possibility of or motivation for betrayal. The valor of courage is seen only against the backdrop of hardship and uncertainty. In short, the height, breadth, and depth of love's expressions expand with imperfection. If we want to have an opportunity to experience the most profound expressions of love, then this world is ideal!

Ironically, we sometimes want the world to be a place where the faintest flicker of faith instantly obliterates everything in life that makes faith a beautiful and courageous choice. The attitude of "I want nirvana and I want it now!" is an emotional response to life, not a reasoned one. It's an attitude that sometimes shows up when people quit smoking or drinking. They expect everyone else to quit, too. Transformations generate such strong feelings that we look for immediate results outside of ourselves. Such sentiments are the type of thinking found in New Year's resolutions. The ends get glorified while the means get despised. But it is valuing the means that allows us to see the glass as half full.

Finding consistency between the concept of a loving God and the state of this world requires us to value the process of accomplishment and be grateful for the opportunity to express extraordinary acts of love. In particular, we must especially value the opportunity to be the architects of our own perfection. There is no reason to assume that we will be stuck in imperfection for all eternity. Such thinking lacks idealism. If the concept of God is to be given fair consideration, then the status of our imperfection should be looked at as the blessing of being given the opportunity to *accomplish* perfection.

There really is nothing like the satisfaction of accomplishment. Anyone can wear a gold metal around chens neck. The glory comes from earning it. Unless the trait is somehow beaten out of us, by nature children want Mommy and Daddy to show them how they can do things for themselves. This disposition is also of great value to us as adults because many of life's greatest satisfactions come from a sense of personal accomplishment. The song *I Did It My Way* was written on earth, not in heaven. If we want to develop a loving attitude, if we want to build strength of character, if we want to achieve a self-motivated transformation from imperfection to perfection, then we are definitely in the right place. By valuing the opportunity to be the creators of our own perfection, imperfection can be appreciated as a reasonable way in which a loving God might create beings with freewill.

IT'S JUST NOT FAIR

✦ ✦ ✦

Mercy for me
Justice for you
I get a second chance
But you get the screw

When the game isn't fair
Don't bother to deal
A pair of double standards
Make God seem unreal

✦ ✦ ✦

Human history is filled with stories of atrocity that bring the goodness of God into question. But who needs history? A good dose of the evening news is all it takes. We watch as deranged high school students gun down classmates by the score or as political unrest unleashes the large-scale horrors of war, and the next thing you know people are proclaiming, "There is no God!" This bespeaks an emotional conflict, not a philosophical one. The heartfelt sentiment is certainly praiseworthy, but the conclusion is unreasoned.

It is not surprising that atrocities are seen as a contradiction to the existence of a loving God because such occurrences beg us to identify with the oppressed. This identification heralds a call for justice. If there is no justice, there is no God. On the other hand, love also admonishes us to temper justice with mercy. The experience of parenting brings this issue to light more clearly than does anything else. As parents, we are called upon to teach and administer the values of justice/fairness and mercy/generosity.[3] Additionally, we are called upon to make decisions about when it is appropriate to intervene in conflicts that our children have with each other and with other people's children.

First, we will examine the tension between justice and mercy. Then we will take on the far more difficult issue of intervention.

And Justice for All

See Moe.
See Moe's brother, Larry.
See Moe and Larry beaming with broad smiles.
That's because even though Moe and Larry only have one joystick between them, they have learned to share.
How could that have possibly happened? Well, they learned it from their Mommy!
"You each get to have a turn for ten minutes," says Mommy. "Then switch."
"I get to go first because I'm smarter, older, stronger, better lookin' than him, and you love me more. Isn't that right Mommy?" implores Moe.

---

[3]Justice is to mercy what fairness is to generosity. Different contexts sometimes call for the use of one pairing of terms rather than the other. Justice and mercy come into play when things have gone wrong. Fairness and generosity are applied to keep things going right. When both of these facets are appropriate to the discussion, I will use the words *justice* and *mercy* for the sake of simplicity.

"Now where would you ever get an idea like that," asks Mommy. "You know I love you both the same. We'll toss a coin. Call it in the air, Moe!"

And that's how Moe and Larry learned to share.

Here comes cousin Curly.

See the sun sparkle on his bald little head as he approaches Moe and Larry's house. Cousin Curly does not have a broad beaming smile. He has a big sad frown because he doesn't have a joystick at his house.

"Let's let cousin Curly play with the joystick for the first half hour because he doesn't get to play as much as you two lucky guys," suggests Mommy.

"But Mommy," screams Moe, "that's not fair! It's our game. Why should Curly get better treatment than your own children? You don't believe in fairness at all. You're just an old wrinkled hag!"

Fairness is easy to teach and hard to argue with. In contrast, mercy is hard to teach and easy to argue with. Moe's harsh words to Mommy demonstrate the common disposition that people have not only for reverting to fairness when the value of applying mercy is not shared, but also for heaping disdain onto those who wish to forsake fairness and manifest mercy. Children must learn justice before they can be taught mercy, and they must learn it through experience. They are hardly sophisticated enough to get the lesson as an intellectual exercise.

When justice isn't present, the natural inclination is to blame the one who is in charge of administering justice. Whether it is Mommy or God, if the administration of justice would make our lives better, it becomes easy to criticize whoever is in charge for being inadequate. Justice is easier to understand than mercy. Justice tends toward being precise, predictable, and socially sanctioned. In contrast, the characteristics of mercy are creativity, imprecision, and individualized expression. We reach out with mercy; we fall back on justice.

Children must learn the value of justice before they can benefit from experiences that teach the value of mercy. Yet as children develop an appreciation for justice, it becomes necessary to extend mercy because mercy helps them develop the nobility of character that manifests as self-correction and tenderness of heart. Tempering justice with mercy is part of the art of living; it cannot be reduced to a formula. All it takes is having more than one child to appreciate that redress for a victim is not more or less important than redeeming an oppressor. When the oppressed and the oppressor, the advantaged and disadvantaged, are both part of the same family, love more easily finds a healthy balance between justice and mercy.

Rather than a blessing, mercy becomes a curse when it is applied before children develop an appreciation for the value of justice. (This is no less true for adults, but addressing the issue becomes a lot more complicated in the absence of a parental authority.) Infants enter the world too unsophisticated to appreciate justice, let alone the attenuation of justice by mercy. In order to instill the value of fairness and the worldly wisdom that "actions have consequences," parents discipline their children; they administer justice. For the purpose of teaching children to have a tender heart regarding the unfairness and imperfections in life and to allow an opportunity for self-correction to occur, parents temper their administration of justice with mercy. The extension of mercy is wise when based on the recognition that there is a reasonable chance that an attitude of self-correction might develop.

Parents have cause to celebrate when their children begin to recognize, admit, and correct their own mistakes. When children begin to develop this level of maturity, the whole tenor of parenting can take on new dimensions. The focus of child rearing evolves from setting healthy boundaries to teaching children how to make wise and creative decisions. As children master fundamental social boundaries, family life can enjoy the ripened fruits of peace, happiness, and accomplishment that are the rewards of successful parenting.

When parents unwisely administer justice or mercy, then everyone in the family suffers for it. Generally speaking, the "spoiled brat" syndrome reflects the over-application of mercy. Children become spoiled when they are sheltered from facing life's worthwhile struggles or from appropriate consequences for inappropriate actions. In contrast, an untrusting and unspirited character often indicates that justice was not sufficiently tempered with mercy. The consequences resulting from the misapplication of justice and mercy manifest in the same way whether the community is the family or the world and whether the stakes are high or low.

When the victim is our own dead child murdered by a stranger, we can easily lose sight of the value of mercy. Questioning the existence of God under such circumstances is natural. Extremes are challenging, but not theologically insurmountable. Notwithstanding that a greater degree of atrocity calls for a greater attenuation of mercy, so also does a heightened ability to rehabilitate an oppressor *and* compensate a victim justify a greater extension of mercy. When considering the redeeming and redressing abilities of God, extreme ministrations of mercy are justifiable. This is especially true given the limitations on divine intervention necessitated by the Freewill Love Factor.

The Mercy of Nonintervention

If there is a God, che has methodologies for teaching justice and mercy that are completely unacceptable for earthly parents to employ. The appropriateness of divine intervention operates on such a different level than it does for earthly parents that it is easy to lose sight of how the same principles are in operation.

Today is a special day. It's Christmas!

See Moe and Larry playing with the only toy they found under the Christmas tree this year. It's a brand new GI Joe!

Moe wants to dress up GI Joe in sand-colored fatigues. He wants to re-create the Desert Storm operation. All the burning oil wells looked so spectacular on television.

Larry wants to dress up GI Joe in camouflage fatigues and pretend to invade Serbia with an infantry division. Ground conflicts seem a lot more exciting than just dropping a bunch of bombs.

See Moe and Larry argue. See them get oh-so-frustrated!

"Let's let Mommy decide," suggests Moe, as he reflects on his imagined most-favored-child status.

"Okay," says Larry, thinking that his interest in current events will carry the day.

"You know, Moe, Desert Storm really is yesterday's news," Mommy says authoritatively. "Focusing on Europe will help you more at school with your current events class. And besides, all that chemical weapons exposure will take the fun out of it."

See Moe and Larry still not getting along. See Moe and Larry go back to Mommy five minutes later with another problem.

"Mommy, Larry keeps talking in a French accent because he doesn't know what Serbs sound like. Please make him stop. It's ruining the whole ambiance!"

"Moe's right, Larry," says Mommy. "At

least try to use the right accent. Listen to the news if you have to. A French accent is no substitute for a Serbian accent. You'll confuse the troops! Now run along and play. Mommy's got work to do."

See Moe and Larry still not getting along. See Moe and Larry come back again in just two minutes. They have learned to bring all their problems to Mommy so that she can sort out each and every conflict that arises between them.

Today is a special day. It's Christmas, again.

Moe and Larry got two new toys for Christmas this year and they're even better than action figures. But the toys are not all that is new at their house. The family is also enjoying a new lesson that they got last year from playing with GI Joe.

"From now on," says Mommy, "you boys work out your own problems. I tried my best last year to teach you how to play nicely together. This year I want you to help Mommy stay out of the psych ward by solving your own problems. Okay? Now open your present and see what Mommy got you for Christmas this year!"

See Moe and Larry ripping through the wrapping paper. See Moe and Larry pull out a slingshot and a brand new pump-action pellet gun. What fun!

"I get to play with the pellet gun first," asserts Moe. Watch Moe load up the gun with pellets and give it a few extra pumps beyond the manufacturer's recommendation.

"Hey, don't be pointing that thing at me," demands Larry.

"Don't be such a baby," snaps Moe. "It's not

like I shot you."

"Then I suppose you won't mind if a few rocks go whizzing past your ear. As long as they don't hit you, there's no damage done. Right?" retorts Larry.

See Mommy take the boys to the hospital. See Mommy reconsider the issue of intervention. It's all fun and games until someone loses an eye.

As adults who embrace love as the highest value, we want others to extend mercy to us so that we may have an opportunity to recognize our mistakes and correct them. Just as we strive to help children see and correct their mistakes, we expect this same consideration from others. Often the extension of mercy means that someone who has already suffered unjustly is being asked to endure further suffering for the sake of tempering justice with mercy. Balancing parental intervention with giving children an opportunity to learn to get along on their own is one of the great challenges of parenthood. Children can do physical harm to each other, and parents, when administering discipline, can do physical harm to their children. In either situation, the degree of harm marks the difference between child rearing and child abuse.[4]

Parents sometimes tolerate one child being abusive toward another. This is not because parents are willing to sacrifice one child to another *just* for the sake of giving the offending one a chance to repent. While the oppressor is given a chance for self-correction, the oppressed child has an opportunity to develop a noble character. Adversity provides the necessary circumstances for learning to express increasingly excellent

---

[4]There are, of course, instances when parents should intervene even though physical harm is not at issue. But when it comes to considering whether this world is a contradiction to the existence of God, it's the sticks and stones far more than the names that people complain about. For this reason, the discussion will be limited to the material world, rather than psychological issues.

acts of love. Learning the value of mercy comes from having it extended to us and from extending it to others.

As parents, we suffer the injustice inflicted upon one child by another for the sake of teaching mercy to both. The wisdom of nonintervention is conditioned by the degree to which physical harm has occurred or might occur. The physical harm standard that is appropriate for measuring our parental wisdom, however, is not appropriate for trying to discern divine wisdom regarding nonintervention.

As parents, we are responsible for caring for our children until they become adults. Once children reach adulthood, if one hits the other, then it is the government's job to step in. The emancipation of children terminates the rights and responsibilities of parenthood. When children reach the governmentally prescribed age of adulthood, they attain a social status that is equal to that of their parents, even though on a personal level the parent-child dynamic may continue to exist.

In contrast, the progressive development of our relationship to a Divine Parent would have radically different characteristics than those associated with biological parents. With God, duration is not limited, equality of social status is never achieved, and (as many a martyr might tell us) the citadel of spiritual freewill is unassailable—one can enjoy inner peace even while enduring outward persecution.

As contrasted with the limitations of biological parents, God presumably can make everything work out in the end through the creation of an afterlife. The wise bestowal of mercy must take into account the time element needed for self-correction and also the harm done by the time lag of justice. Although balancing justice and mercy on a divine scale might look very different than when it is done on a human scale, the principles are the same.

The conditions that make mercy necessary are also the conditions that generate the possibility for such character traits as altruism, loyalty, and courage. The Freewill Love Factor necessitates some degree of suffering. The ministration of mercy means that suffering may increase and be prolonged. But the suffering that comes from human atrocities is a reflection on the character of the people who carry out such atrocities; it should not be permitted to taint the concept of God. If there is *the possibility* that with enough time and a good attitude on our part a God could help us become enriched from even the worst experiences, then to ask for more would be unreasonable. To ask for more would deteriorate the integrity of our freewill because it would produce a Selfish Sam type of experience.

The admonition to take responsibility for one's attitude when faced with terrible injustice does not reflect insensitivity to the plight of the oppressed; it is the rallying cry of spiritual freewill and it glorifies the value of mercy. What is truly insensitive to the human spirit is suggesting that some of us simply are not capable of meeting life's challenges with a positive attitude. This world is filled with plenty of stories about people unpredictably rising to the occasion. Sometimes the ones most surprised are the family and friends of the one plagued by adversity. Other times it is the unfortunate person, chenself, who is most surprised. When we take ownership of our attitude, we open ourselves to the inspiration that can come from anecdotes about how others have bravely met life's challenges. By identifying with the self-empowerment of others, we better realize the spiritual heights to which we can also ascend.

It is contradictory to believe in the existence of God and yet hold that human potential is too limited to *eventually* make the best out of all that comes our way. History is a wonderful thing because even though the events cannot be changed, our interpretation of them can be. By appreciating the necessities of the Freewill Love Factor and by continually upgrading our interpretation of past events, we enable ourselves to not only make peace with the past, but also to find new ways of being enriched by the past. Faith provides an opportunity to make peace with the past and have a positive attitude about the future.

WHAT EVIL LURKS?

✦ ✦ ✦

I see the shadow of evil
No matter where I go
It haunts me like a curse
Like there's something I don't know

It changes shape so quickly
It's every shade but bright
It has only form, not substance
And gives nothing but a fright.

"Your absent mind's forgetting
To turn on your inner light!
Stop your fussing. Just turn it on,"
That's mom—she's always right!

✦ ✦ ✦

Chapter 14 (*Is Imperfection a Good Idea?*) addressed the propriety of creating imperfection on purpose. The conclusion was that intentionally creating imperfection is not incongruous with the existence of God because imperfect environments allow for the most profound expressions of love. The previous chapter, *It's Just Not Fair*, exposed how imperfection necessitates the tempering of justice with mercy.

These two chapters were about finding meaning and value in the inherent conditions of our environment. This chapter addresses the problem of evil as a personal experience. Here, the focus is on accepting responsibility for our inner life by owning our interpretations of events.

In philosophy the problem of reconciling the existence of evil with the existence of God may be an ageless paradox, but in life it is an ever-present spiritual imperative. Thoughts about evil do not work to invalidate faith nearly so much as the experience of it. The conditions of this world scream for an answer to the question of why an all-powerful and loving God couldn't find a way that works better than this (without undermining our freewill). The level of human atrocity and suffering that has seared the body of human history seems "needless." Needless suffering is evil; a loving, omnipotent God would do better. Ergo, there is no God.

The world is ripe with circumstances that encourage second-guessing the wisdom of God. We do need more creative solutions to life's challenges. But the lack of creativity is a case of personal projection dumped on God. When we cannot imagine how the circumstances of life might work together for a greater good, this becomes a reason to question the existence of God.

The problem is looking at the experience of suffering within too short a time frame. All suffering is acceptable if there is sufficient time to make the best of it. Time is not an issue when considering the existence of an eternal God who can provide us with life after death. We can embrace suffering when there is an expectation of future reward. We do this all the time.

Suffering for the sake of a future reward is the mark of maturity. We do this not just in terms of securing the necessities of life, but for the sake of luxuries as well. "If I work enough voluntary overtime now, I'll be able to afford the ski boat I've always wanted." The cost-benefit analysis is highly subjective, of course, as well as what is considered a benefit, but the willingness to embrace opportunities that require a certain degree of suffering is universal.

Our appreciation of how rewards develop out of enduring hardship is not restricted to suffering that is intentionally inflicted. It is common to look back on unpleasant experiences and marvel at how much was learned from them. This does not mean that we wish such experiences on others. Of course not. However, there is a certain quality of character development that comes from facing hardship with dignity, especially when the suffering is not chosen. When one has the determination to use suffering, past or present, as a vehicle for building a noble character, then the rewards of such character growth are available for the rest of one's life.

The point is not to rehash what was stated earlier on the value of participating in the process of perfection. The issue here is one of owning our interpretations of good and evil and acknowledging that our inability to see how things can work out for the best is a personal limitation. When we take personal responsibility for the definitions of good and evil, and when this is done as a part of faith in God, then adversity that would otherwise tempt us to reject faith becomes an opportunity to examine one's commitment to living faithfully. When trust, hope, and loyalty become expressions of faith, adversity can be savored as an opportunity for the dynamic expression of love. Suffering which tempts the rejection of faith becomes nothing more than a window into one's current status of spiritual growth, a vantage point for assessing how faith can be made more whole. The recognition of incomplete faith is a blessing to those who strive to live a wholehearted, life-long commitment to faith in God.

Counting blessings and searching diligently for the good in all experiences is not a cop-out; it is a living affirmation of trust that the ends not only justify the means, but also glorify them.

The Freewill Love Factor necessitates approaching God through faith. Faith requires an attitude of hope and trust

that all things can work together for good. Hope and trust
are logical extensions of believing in a God who is
benevolent, omniscient, and omnipotent. Yet, hoping and
trusting that life will be better in the future does not create an
appreciation for the value of the present. Hope and trust may
make us feel better, but they do not offer intellectual
satisfaction. They do not explain *how* the process works. This
can be understood by appreciating that, as a collective, our
experience of love involves issues of both quantity and
quality. The sport of diving provides a useful analogy.

A diver may execute a perfect swan dive off the low
board and receive a quality value of ten from the judges. The
level (quantity) of difficulty, however, may only have a value
of one. If the value of the dive is measured by multiplying
the quality and quantity, then a perfect swan dive only gets a
score of ten. Another diver may try a triple back flip with a
full twist off the high board. Let's say the difficulty of this
dive has a value of eight. Even a poor-quality dive, one that
only scores a three for execution, yields a score of twenty-four
for the dive.

Now consider the possibility of a world where everyone
just happens to always choose good over evil. Everyone
speaks the truth and does the right thing. Life is good, and
the quantity of people participating is one hundred percent.
But, the strength of character meter (quality) is barely
registering. Forgiveness is never necessary because everyone
always has a wholesome attitude. Loyalty has never really
been tested because no one has the experience of ever being
betrayed. Altruism is hard to express when everything is fair
and everyone cooperates so nicely. This world, where
spiritual *quantity* has been maximized, eliminates the
opportunity for the type of high quality spiritual experience
that comes only through tribulation.

This, of course, is not an excuse to pray that others screw
up so that we can enjoy the rewards of greater personal
spiritual growth. However, by recognizing that our
individual potentials are augmented by the mistakes of

others, we lose the right to complain about how the mistakes of others *unfairly* cause us to suffer. As well, if humanity as a whole eventually ends up with a higher score on the nobility-of-character scale, then God should be off the hook for not creating a better world. Holding love as the highest value leads to the desire to maximize the *quantity* of people who are doing good. This is how we love humanity as a whole. As individuals (and as a group of individuals), quality achievements compensate for the suffering occasioned by natural forces and the evil acts of others. This trade-off of the quality-quantity issue creates the cosmic balance that justifies the experience of imperfection in all of its forms.

When we consider the possibility that God could provide future benefits to compensate for an initially harsh environment, then we can begin to see how the suffering of this world cannot be a reason for denying the existence of God. On one end of the spectrum, we have the extremely primitive state in which humans first existed; on the other end of the spectrum is the achievement of Utopia. Every step in between these two states must be appreciated as providing the potential for a worthwhile experience, both individually and collectively. This appreciation reflects a reasoned understanding of the trust that is a necessary component of having whole-hearted faith in God. This perspective works to encourage those with faith in God to savor the particular challenges that come their way and to be all the more grateful for the advances in culture and civilization that are the gift of previous generations.

IT'S A MATTER OF PROOF

✦ ✦ ✦

The mystery of life isn't a problem to solve
but a reality to experience.
Frank Herbert

✦ ✦ ✦

If we had proof of God's existence, it would do our lives
more harm than good because of the Freewill Love Factor.
Objective proof would undermine our ability to know that
love is real. How the proof is offered is not the issue. Proof
undermines freewill whether it comes through a compelling
line of logic or a revelatory experience such as Selfish Sam
had. Even if one person's experience of God could somehow
be satisfactorily offered to another, the principle of the
Freewill Love Factor is violated just the same.

Proving the existence of God to one's self, however, is an
entirely different matter. As we travel down the road of faith,
progressive revelations of the reality of God do not
undermine our freewill. Though a proof of God based on
logic would undermine freewill, personal experience of God
through faith does not necessarily undermine freewill or our
ability to know that our love is real.

Experience, as well as logic, can provide us with a sense

of security about what is real. By recognizing when to turn to experience, rather than logic, for our understanding of life, we can make a graceful transition from belief in God to knowledge of God without disrespecting the Freewill Love Factor. Just as the reality of love can be appreciated through personal experience (notwithstanding the fact that the definition of love is alogical), so also can experience provide a personal knowledge of God, even though such knowledge is not transferable. Logic is of limited value when pondering the existence of God because logic can be shared. Personal experience, on the other hand, is not transferable. If experience provides knowledge of God for one person, this does not mean it has provided knowledge of God for anyone else.

The question "What if we are just brains in a vat?" was used earlier to demonstrate the philosophic difficulty of making any claim to knowledge. The distinction between the methodology used for attaining secular knowledge as compared with spiritual knowledge was explored, as well. These concepts are useful for appreciating how a transition from *belief* in God to *knowledge* of God can be a gradual and evolving process. When we remember that knowledge is not an absolute and when we are self-reliant in our quest for spiritual knowledge, then a gradual and increasingly compelling experience of God becomes a *possibility*. By looking to the blossoming of our individual spiritual experience for the validation of faith, we hold the key that opens the door to transcending the limitations of the Freewill Love Factor.

People of faith often speak of feeling the presence of God or believing that God protected them in an emergency. Some people report being healed; others speak of an indescribable inner knowing. Of course, this does nothing to prove the existence of God, but if such occurrences were not reported, they would be conspicuous for their absence. If our love is real and if faith opens the door to having experiences with God, then it should be progressively safer for us to experience

God without such experience undermining freewill. If God is "distant" out of respect for our freewill, then as love liberates us from the Freewill Love Factor, more experiences of God should develop.

How such experiences emerge in the course of any one individual's faith-journey is an extremely personal matter, and not surprisingly, often such experience is described as too deep for words. But how experience with God has been described throughout time and across religious cultures is consistent with what should happen if there is a God. I am not suggesting that this does anything to prove the existence of God. Nonetheless, noting how human experience complements theism is important because if it did not, this would legitimately call into question whether reality is inconsistent with the speculation that God exists. The internal consistency of theism is complemented by human experience. And at this point, the internal consistency of theism is all that is being suggested.

PART IV

RECOGNIZING THE POSSIBILITIES

At this point we have covered the ground
necessary to show that the concept of God is
not inconsistent with the conditions of this world
and that the existence of God is plausible. The
next step is to compare atheism, agnosticism,
and theism (the "gnostic paradigms") as three
internally consistent but mutually exclusive
paradigms. We will start with an analogy
between the gnostic paradigms and the three
geometric models for mapping three-
dimensional space. No previous understanding
of these geometric models is necessary, and
what needs to be explained is easily
understood! The first chapter in Part IV
explains everything you need to know about
the geometric models for the purpose of
comparing them to the gnostic paradigms. The
second chapter in Part IV compares choosing a
geometric model for a particular application
with selecting between which gnostic paradigm
we will apply to our daily lives.

THE GEOMETRY ANALOGY

✦ · ✦ ✦

John the Builder, architect for the Tower of Babel[5], was calmly introspective as the workers, speaking incomprehensibly to each other, left the construction site. The foreman, David, was nonplussed. In exasperation he turned to John and said, "We hoped this would bring us into the presence of God, but instead our search for God has only incurred his wrath. Are you not even the least bit disturbed to watch all that we have dreamed of creating be laid to waste?"

"This is not God's wrath," admonished John. "Rather, it is his loving protection. Our reach now exceeds our grasp. But one day, when we have more fully grown as a people, we shall experience what we now seek. The nourishment of meat is not given to babies, nor does God allow us to experience greater spiritual stature before we can gracefully experience the lesser state.

---

[5]The story of the Tower of Babel comes from the Old Testament. It says that at the dawn of human history everyone spoke the same language. The people tried to build a tower high enough to reach God. For the presumptuousness of their endeavor, God punished them by making them each speak a different language. See Genesis 11:4-9.

"Besides, God has still left us with one
language in common—the very language by which I
conceived this enterprise. To some degree, we all
still speak the language of mathematics. Someday,
when we build with greater love than we have
available to us today, this language will once again
be used to complete that which we have started."

✦   ✦   ✦

One of the beauties of mathematics is that once we
understand the language, it does not tend to suffer
misinterpretation. Though the language of mathematics is
limited in scope, within its circumscribed realm, we enjoy a
precision of mutual understanding that is not found with any
other form of communication. Because mathematics enjoys
such universally consistent interpretation, this language
provides the potential for creating wonderfully precise
analogies. This precision is especially useful for considering
content that is highly subjective and easily misinterpreted. For
this reason, the language of mathematics, more specifically the
field of geometry, will be used to clarify the nature of our
relationship to the gnostic paradigms—atheism, agnosticism,
and theism.

In geometry there are three different models for mapping
three-dimensional space. Using these models to understand
the gnostic paradigms is valuable because just as the existence
of God cannot be proven, neither can it be shown that any one
of the geometric models reflects objective reality better than the
other two. In order to appreciate the analogy, only an
elementary understanding of these geometric models is
necessary. This will not be the least bit complicated. Anyone
left with emotional scars from a past course in geometry will
not have to relive those horrors!

First, let's look at plane geometry. Plane geometry uses the
"x," "y," and "z" axes for the purpose of mapping three-
dimensional space. The "x" and "y" axes create the horizontal

plane by quantifying breadth and depth. The "z" axis quantifies the dimension of height. (See Illustration 1.)

Axioms are propositions that are accepted as true without proof for the sake of studying the consequences that follow from them. There are certain axioms associated with plane geometry. From this set of axioms, certain things can be deduced. For instance, using the axioms of plane geometry, we can deduce that the sum of the angles of any triangle will always equal exactly 180°. Plane geometry works great for activities such as framing a house. As long as the distances involved do not approach global or universal proportions, getting out your protractor and measuring the angles of any triangle will always yield a sum of 180°. (See Illustration 2.)

Another type of geometry is called spherical geometry. When distances reach global proportions (or when a sphere is being used to represent a plane), measurements yield results consistent with spherical geometry. Here the plane is defined not by an "x," "y," intersection of axes, but rather by specifying a point and a radius. By rotating the radius in all directions around the point, a plane is defined in the shape of a sphere. Different planes can be defined by lengthening or shortening the radius. (See Illustration 3.) From the axioms of spherical geometry, we can deduce that all triangles will have more than 180°. Consider a globe. Starting at the North Pole, imagine a line going down to the equator; travel any distance along the equator, then head back up to the North Pole. Note that the two angles from the equator up to the North Pole each equal 90°. Therefore, the total number of degrees in this triangle will be 180° plus the number of degrees in the angle at the North Pole. If we are sailing around the world or otherwise using the surface of a sphere as a plane, then the axioms of spherical geometry are very well suited to our needs. (See Illustration 4.)

The third type of geometry is called hyperbolic geometry. Hyperbolic geometry defines the plane as the interior points of a circle. The interior points of a sphere define three-dimensional space. In this geometric model, distance is

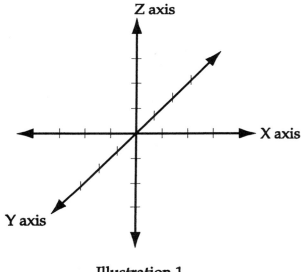

Illustration 1

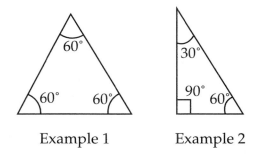

Example 1   Example 2

Illustration 2

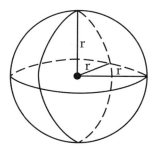

A sphere with a one inch radius.

r = one inch

Illustration 3

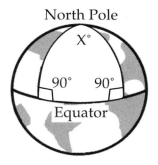

Illustration 4

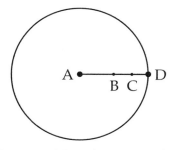

distance AB = distance BC

Illustration 5

"compacted" as you get closer to the outer edge. To see how this works, we need to define four points. The first point, *A*, will be the center. The second point, *D*, will be a point on the edge of the circle. The third point, *B*, will be at the midpoint between A and D. And the fourth point, *C*, will be the midpoint between B and D. In hyperbolic geometry, the distance between A and B is understood to equal the distance between B and C. Distances become condensed as we approach the edge of the circle. (See Illustration 5.) In this geometry, all triangles have less than 180°. When measuring distances that approach and exceed galactic proportion, the measurements will be consistent with hyperbolic geometry.

The important thing to remember about these geometric models is that even though each one is internally consistent, they are also mutually exclusive. Due to the way terms are defined, there can be no common language between them once one has chosen to use a particular model. Although the concept of the triangle exists in each of the three models, an actual triangle is quite different in each model. A triangle must have 180°, more than 180° or less than 180°; these concepts cannot be combined in any meaningful way.

At this point, all we have done is to think abstractly about the different geometric models. We have not applied them to any real world situation (and we're not going to). The preceding discussion has been a metalanguage discussion—a language used for the purpose of explaining the three different languages of the geometric models.

Having developed a sufficient appreciation of the three geometric models that can be used for mapping spatial relationships, we can now compare and contrast these models with the gnostic paradigms.

The first similarity is that both the geometric models and the gnostic paradigms, as collectives, are comprehensive, all-inclusive, and mutually exclusive. The geometric models are comprehensive in that they each fully satisfy the requirements for mathematically mapping the coordinates of three-dimensional space. The gnostic paradigms address our fundamental relationship to life as it relates to the nature of objective reality; this is as comprehensive as comprehensive gets. The geometric models are all-inclusive in that neither real world experience nor abstract reasoning suggests that any other comprehensive geometric models exist. The gnostic paradigms are all-inclusive because, given the question of whether God exists, "yes," "no," and "I don't know" exhaust the possible answers to that question. The mutually exclusive nature of the geometric models has already been addressed. The mutually exclusive nature of "yes," "no," and "I don't know" is self-evident.

The second similarity is that the three geometric models and the three gnostic paradigms are each internally consistent. The internal consistency of the gnostic paradigms is admittedly not open to the same objective scrutiny that can be used for analyzing the geometric models. The ideas that have been presented in support of the internal consistency of theism cannot hope to attain the level of consensual appreciation attained with the geometric models. Additionally, as was stated in the introduction, the internal consistency of atheism and agnosticism is being assumed. For these reasons, the assumption of internal consistency for the gnostic paradigms may at first seem like too large a *philosophic* leap, one that can seriously weaken the analogy being made to the geometric models.

What we are looking at here, however, are choices about issues that cannot be proven. The only assumption is that people choose for themselves the paradigm that they find to be reasonably consistent with their view of life. Therefore, there is not a huge philosophic leap being taken by assuming the internal consistency of atheism and agnosticism. Rather, we are merely accepting that these positions are adopted by some and that for those who hold such positions, the internal consistency of these positions is personally sufficient.

As for the internal consistency of theism, the question is not one of whether the material presented here satisfies the mind of everyone who holds a doctoral degree in philosophy. This is no time to look to "experts" for an answer. (Nor am I suggesting that you approach this material any less critically than someone who holds a doctoral degree in philosophy.) What matters is that, for whatever reasons, *you* are satisfied with the internal consistency of theism. It is *your experience* and *your reasoning* that are relevant. Because of the alogical and subjective nature of some of the concepts associated with theism, and because of the profoundly personal nature of this aspect of our lives, it is imperative to apply all of our tools for understanding—logic, intuition, and experience.

The third and most important similarity between the geometric models and the gnostic paradigms is that no logical proof can establish any of them as representing objective reality. Therefore, the choice to use one of the geometric models or to choose one of the gnostic paradigms is based solely on personal considerations. There are no constraints, no requirements. Freewill reigns supreme. *Subjective values determine the direction we take.*

In some ways, however, choosing between the gnostic paradigms is exactly the opposite of choosing to apply one of the geometric models. For starters, in life we do not have the luxury of engaging in a metalanguage discussion as we can with the geometric models. We can talk about the models theoretically because we are not obliged to apply them to any particular situation. Because we do not have to be constantly applying the geometric models, we can engage in a metalanguage discussion about them. Our lives, however, are always applied lives. Life is not suspended while we ponder the nature of our existence.

Even agnosticism, which superficially appears to be a "non choice," really is a choice. Agnosticism suggests that it would be unwise to take a position on the subject of God's existence. This reflects a subjective interpretation and evaluation of life experience and, as such, is a manifestation of freewill choice. Because we have been inquiring into the wisdom of having faith in God, the language of agnosticism (the "I don't know" language) has been the language of choice.

The implication of this is that *our experience of life is conditioned by our choice.* Interpretations and evaluations of life experience are conditioned by the gnostic paradigm we choose to live in. This is completely dissimilar to consideration of the geometric models because they do not effect our interpretive experience of the essence and meaning of life. Geometric models are tools; theistic paradigms are a way of life.

The challenge with the geometric models is choosing which one will be easiest to apply in a given situation. There is no reason to pick any one of the geometric models as most representative of objective reality. Even though they are mutually exclusive on a paradigmatic level, on a practical level the value of each one can be enjoyed simultaneously. Their mutually exclusive nature does not diminish their independent value. Even if science proved one of the models to be the most accurate reflection of objective reality, we would still use one of the others when a particular application called for it. When that application was over, we would proceed with our lives happy that someone else had figured out the equations so that all we had to do was plug in the numbers.

Bouncing around between the gnostic paradigms on a daily basis is not so satisfying as jumping from one geometric model to the next. Unlike the geometric models, the gnostic paradigms are interpretive responses related to the essence and meaning of life. Even agnosticism is an applied wisdom. The gnostic paradigms take on the psychological dynamics of knowledge because they *are* applied wisdom. Consequently, there is a lot more at stake in choosing between gnostic paradigms than geometric models. The mutually exclusive nature of the gnostic paradigms makes it terribly hard on the psyche to vacillate between them. With the geometric models, the value of one does not exclude the value of the others. With the gnostic paradigms, to live by one we must personally (though not necessarily intellectually) forsake the value of the other two.

COMPETING PARADIGMS

✦ ✦ ✦

Carrie and Terri are twin sisters who love collecting stuffed animals. After making their beds in the morning, they carefully arrange these furry friends on their respective beds.

One day their mother came in and said they would soon be leaving for Grandma's house.

"You can each bring one of your stuffed animals for the car ride. We have to leave in a few minutes. So, hurry up and choose," warned their mother. "When I come back in this room, it's going to be time to go to Grandma's whether or not you've decided which one to bring."

Carrie and Terri had recently become very melodramatic about choosing between furry friends. What if it turned out to be the last ride of their young lives!?! Would the courage of Simba, the Lion King, or the Zen-wisdom of Pooh escort them to the great beyond? Narrowing it down to just one was such a hard choice.

When their mother came back in the room, she found Terri sitting on the bed staring through tears at all of her animals. She was paralyzed by indecision. Carrie, for the first time, did not share Terri's frustration. She sat happily on the bed hugging

Simba with all her might. Strewn on the floor around her were all of the other stuffed animals.

"Usually you get as frustrated as Terri. How did you decide so quickly and happily?" their mother asked Carrie.

"Well, this time I started by figuring out which one was my least favorite," stated Carrie very matter-of-factly. When I decided which one was my least favorite, I threw it on the floor. That way it wasn't around to confuse me and make the decision harder than it needed to be. I kept using this process to narrow down the options. As I got rid of the ones that I knew were not my favorite, I saw that the choices I had left looked better and better. For some reason deciding what was not my favorite was less difficult that trying to figure out which one was my favorite."

✦ ✦ ✦

We choose a geometric model based on our previously chosen application. Once the application is chosen, we can apply only one model at a time. We cannot mix and match axioms and maintain intellectual integrity. Similarly, consistency demands that we choose between the gnostic paradigms of atheism, agnosticism, and theism based on which one is most complementary to and consistent with our previously chosen value of love. To enjoy the freedom to choose between the gnostic paradigms, we must be able see each of them as each internally consistent and as not unreasonable. When we reach this point, we can be guided by the supreme value of love in making the best choice.

With the geometric models, a specific problem or circumstance guides us in which model to choose. Maybe we want to sail the world or maybe our math teacher is passing out an exam that covers six weeks of plane geometry, but something comes along to get us out of the metalanguage discussion and into application. When we are done with the application, it has not changed our experience of reality. Previous and satisfying experiences with a particular geometric model do not predispose us to misapply it to new situations that call for a different model. Moving between geometric models is easy and comfortable because these models are nothing more than tools.

Along with a given geometric model come the axioms of that model. In plane geometry the sum of the angles of a triangle is always exactly 180°. So long as we work with the axioms, we get the correct answers. Getting the right answer is everything. Consequently, once a geometric model has been chosen for a given application, we readily accept the axioms that are appropriate for that model.

Unlike the geometric models, the gnostic paradigms should not be chosen based on a specific situation. These paradigms are supposed to be applicable to all situations. Therefore, individual experience is of limited value, except to the degree that it takes on a universal quality. Experiences that are common to most everyone are useful for understanding our general condition, and this is important for developing beliefs about life and its meaning.

With the geometric models, there is a safe harbor of metalanguage to retreat to when we are not forced to sail the seas of real mathematical living. With the gnostic paradigms, we are always swimming in the gnostic sea of our choice. With math, sometimes we can get out of doing the problem. We can trade bubble gum for homework assignments. But no one else can live our life for us. We are always living within a gnostic paradigm. The only question is whether at any given moment we care to choose a different one.

Because we are always living "applied" lives, we must accept the logical consequences of choosing to be atheistic, agnostic, or theistic. Just as with the geometric models, each gnostic paradigm has inherent limitations and features. If we believe that God does not exist, then nothing in our experience can be interpreted as a manifestation of God's existence. According to our self-imposed definition of life experience, such a possibility does not exist. If we are agnostic, then in theory, there could be an experience that proves the existence of God. However, such an experience would not respect the Freewill Love Factor. Therefore, there can be no hope of such proof. Consequently, all experience will be interpreted as insufficient grounds for taking a position. If we are theists, then all experiences manifest God to some degree and, therefore, validate that choice.

This circularity between belief and interpretation of experience is the natural result of entering into realms where no combination of reasoning and experience can offer objective proof. When we are faced with comprehensive, mutually exclusive, internally consistent paradigms and models, then the value of choosing any one of the possible paradigms or models is personal. The geometric models are user-friendly in the sense that we can sit back and engage in a metalanguage discussion until the cows come home. Or if we care to apply a model, everyone can get out their protractor and come up with the same measurements. But there is one huge drawback to the geometric models: they are not very useful for understanding life and the meaning of it all (unless we get clever and try to analogize them to gnostic paradigms, which is the most practical application I ever found for this stuff).

With the gnostic paradigms, we are not afforded the luxury of a metalanguage chat room. Like rats in the lab, we are trapped in the maze of our lives. Whether or not we believe we can find the Big Cheese, the clock ticks just as loud. And to make matters worse, even if we find the Big Cheese, we are not really able to lead anyone else there. But even though we have nothing more than our own subjective experience to rely on, at least the gnostic paradigms are as comprehensive as comprehensive gets.

It is no great loss that the subjective nature of spiritual experience does not permit its objective verification. In fact, this is a blessing when love is the highest value because the Freewill Love Factor provides an opportunity to know that our love is real. And faith provides the trust and hope that the freewill-respecting limitations on revelations of God will be progressively transcended.

The subjective interpretation of experience is just as subjective, just as personally arbitrary, whether one is an atheist, agnostic, or theist. Ownership of our assessment of life allows us to appreciate that we affect our ability to interpret our experiences just as profoundly no matter which gnostic paradigm we choose.

PART V

THE LEAP:
BELIEVING WITHOUT KNOWING

Parts I, II and III worked together to develop a concept of God that is internally consistent with our experience of life. Part IV focused on the nature of our choice between the gnostic paradigms. Part V is about what it takes to make that choice. The first two chapters in Part V are about appreciating the profundity of making the choice to have faith in God and about leaving behind our emotional baggage as we prepare to make that decision. This is followed by an application of the value of love to the decision-making process and an exploration of what beliefs are *minimally* necessary for the full liberation of love. Part V concludes with an invitation to join the family of the faith-children of God. This is not an invitation to join a religion. It is an invitation to share an experience of spiritual identity.

THE NATURE OF FAITH AS A CHOICE

✦ ✦ ✦

If I bet my life on the Chicago Bulls[6]
Just for argument's sake
The problem is not with choosing the Bulls
But with how much I put at stake

On the other hand, if I go with God
I must wager just the same
But at least I don't just sit and watch
I get to play the game.

✦ ✦ ✦

The degree to which one's spiritual faith begins with a mix of selfish and selfless motivations is not important. All faith starts out less than perfect, and on most days life does not test faith very severely. Nonetheless, just because faith is not being immediately tested does not mean that it is not whole-hearted. Though not every moment tests our ability to faithfully sail the stormy winds of adversity, every moment

---

[6]For those unfamiliar with professional basketball, the Chicago Bulls won six national championships between 1991 and 1998.

does bring an opportunity for renewed faith, a sincere rededication of idealistic intention. Re-affirmation of faith is not really any different than the first affirmation of faith, except for one progressively important factor: *experience*. The first step is always the hardest and should be respected as such.

Part I, *Defining Love, Logic, Freewill, and God*, worked to develop an understanding of how the Freewill Love Factor requires initial protection from a full revelation of God in order to safeguard our freewill and provide us an opportunity to experience the reality of love. Part II, *Faith*, explained how humanity's commonly claimed experiences of the divine are consistent with a theistic paradigm; by living faithfully, we can transcend the Freewill Love Factor. Additionally, the relationship between belief and knowledge in a spiritual context and issues relating to the emotional dynamics of spiritual faith were explored. That section showed how spiritual faith is a process of continual re-affirmation, rather than a single decision made for a lifetime.

By the force of freewill, faith forms the foundation of our relationship to each other and holds the hope of experiencing the love of God. But the fulfillment of faith comes from constant commitment. If our hands are not steadied by sincerity, we risk cutting ourselves on the serrated edge of a life lived with dubious direction. If faith is anything less than a lifetime of re-affirmed intention, then it is nothing.

Nonetheless, the journey of faith does begin somewhere. Since the first step of faith redefines *who* we are, it is hardly surprising that such a step is sometimes referred to as a rebirth. The first step is a lulu because it is a paradigm shift. The experience is referred to as *being reborn* for a reason; the transition is as dynamic as leaving the womb. This is why sincere and critical thinking is crucial. Specifically, we need to appreciate that just because we may view theism as an internally consistent paradigm, that does not necessarily make it the best choice. Again, an analogy to the geometric models can be helpful.

The plane geometry model is the easiest one to understand. It is intuitively satisfying for the same reason that people initially thought the world was flat; it is the geometry of proximate experience. Additionally, this model is inviting because it provides answers to certain kinds of questions with less information than do the other models. For instance, if you know two angles of a triangle, then you can figure out the third angle by subtracting the sum of the first two from 180°. There are other examples that also demonstrate how plane geometry has user-friendly qualities that are lacking in the other models. This does not mean, however, that we ought to always use plane geometry or believe that it reflects objective reality. In order to justify such a position, there would have to be a lifelong application, one overriding purpose.

The quality of being internally consistent only makes an option plausible; it only opens up a choice. Whether one choice is better than another is a separate question. The theistic paradigm must also best support love if it is to lead us to the conclusion that we ought to have faith. Just as with the geometric models where appropriate choice is determined by the specific application, with the gnostic paradigms, the decision should be based on which choice best supports our highest value—love. It is not enough to simply *want* to have faith in God; there must also be a reason why we *ought* to have faith in God.

FREEING ONE'S SELF
FROM PAST EXPERIENCE

✦ ✦ ✦

Don't let what you're being get in the way
of what you might become.
Harry Palmer

✦ ✦ ✦

Deciding to have faith in God is not like any other
decision. Faith defines the nature of one's existence and
establishes a moral and ethical framework for relating to
other people. It offers the ultimate carrot: the invitation to
personally know God and to experience receiving God's love.
And all it asks in return is a complete identity makeover,
accessorized with beliefs that you'll be expected to pay for
before you're allowed to try them on.

It is fair enough to say that the first step of faith is indeed
a leap. But faith does not have to leap over reason. Faith
does not require us to leave our intellects behind as we begin
to walk the path of spiritual discovery that leads to God. The
first faith-step must be a leap because there are some things
in life that shouldn't be stepped in, but are, nonetheless,
important to get past. Therefore, faith wisely leaps over all

obstacles to love. Faith dares to soar above doubt, uncertainty, and the vast abyss of the alogical. But the biggest hurdle that the initial leap of faith must clear is past experience.

If we are to consider embarking on a relationship with God, then we need to separate the wisdom of our experience from the experiences themselves. If our understanding of faith in God is striving to touch transcendent Truth, then it must have a universal appeal. One way to peer into this perspective is to ask: "Would I reach this same conclusion regardless of my upbringing and environment?" The value in approaching faith this way is that it provides an opportunity for all people to be unified by a common understanding of faith, even though the experience of faith is subjective and often too deep for words. Theology becomes a stumbling block if the definition of faith is not appropriate for all people at all times.

When the understanding of faith in God takes on this type of universal appeal, then the drawing power of faith is eternally secure. Every time the gravity of selfishness pulls us down to the animal level of a more materialistic outlook, faith, like the wind, powerful yet unseen, lifts us up. Faith is both attitude and action. Love-motivated faith liberates hope, validates trust, and justifies idealism. Faith encourages acceptance of ourselves even if our current state of character development is but a faint reflection of that which we strive to be.

LOVE IS THE GREATEST

✦ ✦ ✦

Love bears all things, believes all things,
hopes all things, endures all things.
Love never fails.

There abide faith, hope, and love,
but the greatest of these is love.

Pursue love, yet keep zealously seeking
all of the spiritual gifts.

1 CORINTHIANS 13, 14

✦ ✦ ✦

How can we hold love as the highest value? Let me count the
ways.

We affirm that love is our highest value in life.
We make choices consistent with doing the greatest good, for
the greatest number, for the greatest length of time.
We live for love and are willing to die for it.
We allow others their fair measure of suffering and pleasure as
wisdom dictates, and we graciously accept the same.
We give generously to others as wisdom dictates and
graciously accept the same.

We take care of ourselves so that we have the energy to love.
We express love through both forgiveness and healthy
	boundaries.
We generate and appreciate beauty, truth, and goodness.
We speak, sing, and listen to love.
We believe what is reasonable, if it promotes love.
We hope for love.
We teach love and learn to love.
We learn to love learning to love.
We learn to love learning to love learning to love.
We are physically, intellectually, and spiritually courageous
	when defending the cause of love.
We are loyal to the supreme value of love.
We are not critical of the author for going on and on about
	love, and we laugh out loud at all of his jokes . . .

   It's fun to strike up the band for love. We could sing a few
catchy refrains about how love leads to faith in God and go
home emotionally satisfied. But this is not about being
hypnotically "pied-pipered" into a quick decision. If faith is to
last a lifetime, better that it is entered into with sincere reflection
and our most critical thinking, not simply in response to deeply
felt emotions. Our personal wisdom, the product of our best
synthesis of reason and experience, is the solid foundation on
which to make decisions that cut to the core of who we are and
what we are about.
   Faith in God is not for the faint-hearted or the fickle because
the pursuit of love takes courage no matter which gnostic
paradigm we choose. Faith does not keep one out of trouble,
but it helps to make the most of adversity. "Bottoming out"
sometimes acts as a catalyst for choosing faith, yet where the
journey begins is not nearly so important as where it ends—as
an act of love. Appreciating that wake-up calls can be powerful
catalysts for positive change, however, is no excuse for courting
disaster. Better to approach faith as a courageous act done from
a position of strength. By securely fastening faith to the logic of
love, we can safely celebrate the joys and bravely face the
challenges that faithful living brings.

THE INTEGRITY OF FAITH-BELIEFS

Faith in God has the potential to unify all people. By allowing our faith identity to transcend political and religious identity, we can become better members of both of these institutions. Religious and political institutions have a certain criteria for membership. What defines membership eligibility is where the essence of humanity gets defined. Inasmuch as faith-beliefs define one's relationship to others, this issue directly affects our relationship to religious and political institutions.

Religious and political institutions engage the conflicts of disunity and build the blessings of culture on the field of faith-beliefs. When religious or political disenfranchisement becomes an excuse for the mistreatment of others, then the battle over faith-beliefs has been waged. For instance, a democracy that tolerates the enslavement of a particular race has hardly provided humanity with the full blessings of government. Similarly, a religion so self-referential that it renounces spiritual kinship with anyone who is not a member has hardly provided humanity with the full blessings of spiritual life.

On an institutional level, when religious and political organizations minimize the criteria for membership, this fosters unity. When only adulthood and competency are required, then religious and political institutions have taken the first step toward unifying humanity. As individuals, we can work toward creating interpersonal unity by simplifying faith-beliefs so that love flows freely to all people. As individuals, we wield the power to define faith-beliefs. By our willingness to see all other persons as part of our spiritual family, we create spiritual unity.

Defining God as a creator, a spiritual parent, implies that we are the children of God. This is the first step in generating unifying faith-beliefs. Faith in a spiritual parent identifies one as a child of God. By so formulating our sense of spiritual identity, we can answer the question "Who are we?" with "We are children of God." This creates the universal connection through which the current of love can flow. By defining all of humanity as part of our spiritual family, we have the power, as individuals, to unify ourselves with everyone else. When the only sense of spiritual separation between a person with faith and one without is that they don't *share* a belief in spiritual kinship, then faith-beliefs have worked to maximize our experience of unity.

The integrity of faith-beliefs rests not only on the beauty of their unifying power, but also on their philosophic consistency. Some people, for instance, declare that we are all brothers and sisters, but they do not recognize a parental God. While the desire to express a sense of human unity in such touchingly familiar tones is certainly beautiful, the bastardization of terminology has no better example. It is having a common parent that makes us siblings. Wisdom must be married to love in order to procreate viable faith-beliefs. The sentiment that desires spiritual family must cooperate with the intellect that understands what the word *family* implies.

There is a real challenge in asserting that spiritual kinship is of a higher order than biological kinship, while simultaneously describing spiritual reality in terms of archetypal and idealized biological relationships. When words from our biological relationships are used to describe spiritual relationships, we must endeavor to be as precise and specific as possible. Talking about siblings who have no common parent is like saying someone is just a little bit pregnant. Analogies to biological relationships should not twist the words of biology beyond meaningful recognition, especially since the very existence of spiritual reality is an open question. The ability to appreciate what can only be experienced by faith is needlessly complicated by a poor choice of words.

Saying that we are all spiritual siblings without presuming the existence of a spiritual parent is just one example of how we must be careful not to let sentiment disintegrate the integrity of faith-beliefs. Other examples could be given. The point is simply to show that when faith-beliefs do not withstand critical analysis, they become obstacles to unity because they forsake the value of logic. Logical reasoning is one of our best tools for creating universally appealing faith-beliefs. It must not be abandoned when we need it the most.

Once we are committed to the value of preserving logical consistency, we can explore exactly which faith-beliefs best support the value of love and reflect the goodness of God. If faith is to liberate love, then those beliefs that have the distinction of being faith-beliefs ought to be those that are *minimally* necessary to *fully* liberate love. To accomplish this goal, we must examine the obstacles to love. The two core obstacles are selfishness and spiritual judgment. Selfishness is the antithesis of love, and spiritual judgment is a justification for withholding love.

LOVE IS IN THE PRESENT

✦ ✦ ✦

In God we trust.

✦ ✦ ✦

Love is always experienced in the present because love is simultaneously attitude and action, a way of being as well as a way of doing. (Conversations count as action. That's why prayer and worship provide the faithful with the experience of receiving God's love.) Sometimes when we imagine the future or look back upon the past, we decide that our imagined future or our interpretation of the past is a valid excuse for not loving someone in the present. *Fear* will be used to generally describe a rationalization for selfishness based on possible future events. *Judgment* (meaning spiritual judgment—presuming the right and ability to look into the inner life of another) will be used to generally describe the rationalization for justifying the right to withhold love based on past events.

Spiritual judgment of another is always inappropriate. Posing the question of whether someone is worthy of love is the problem. We can't get a good answer to a bad question. What justifies judging Mother Theresa a saint also justifies judging Hitler a sinner. People are worthy of love not because of how they *act* in the world, but because of who we *are* in the world. The issue isn't accuracy. It's attitude. *Love must be unconditional.* The question is whether we are willing to be spiritual vigilantes. Although vigilantes sometimes get the right person, this does not justify taking the "law" into one's own hands.

By looking at fear and judgment we will see what faith-beliefs are necessary to fully liberate us from these obstacles to love.

Fear: The Seed of Selfishness

Our relationship to mortality eventually becomes either a desert wasteland or the rich soil in which the roots of love can grow most deeply. Whether mortality becomes the excuse for a "me first" attitude or the backdrop for supreme expressions of love is all up to us. There is no sitting on the fence with this one. Without a sense of security about an afterlife, morality is mercilessly subjective, hope is lost, trust is irrational, and the vindication of love is but a fanciful dream of wishful thinkers.

This very same sense of mortality also creates the opportunity for the most supreme expression of love—the willingness to lay down one's life for another. Mortality does not contradict the goodness of God. If love is the highest value, then an environment that stimulates and provides an opportunity for experiencing the most profound manifestations of love is consistent with the concept of a loving God.

Death is our most primal fear and a fundamental inhibitor to the full liberation of love. But the problem is not with the fact of death. The problem is not having a faith-belief that vanquishes the fear of death. In one form or another, almost every religion addresses this issue. From reincarnation to eternal life in heaven, cosmologies have been developed to overcome the fear of death. Some religions also teach that hell awaits those who, having rejected God, must face the final judgment. This type of doctrine must be distinguished from teachings that suggest God practices tough love, that God blesses us with consequences for our actions so that we might learn a better way of living.

There is an important difference between being made to suffer just but loving consequences for misdeeds and suffering punishment for the sake of retribution. Doctrines of eternal damnation play upon selfishness. While they may encourage moral behavior (not to mention any other agendas of the institutions that perpetuate such doctrines), they play on fear rather than inspire love. By playing upon insecurities about mortality, such doctrines may promote good actions, but they invariably undermine the development of a good attitude because they are coercive in nature.

The mercy of God must, of course, be tempered by the justice of God. Knowing all the details of the administration of divine justice, however, is not necessary for the adoption of faith-beliefs that liberate love. Our task is to determine which beliefs (consistent with love as the highest value) are minimally necessary to fully liberate love. We are not required to take a position on the fate of those who do not choose to hold love as the highest value.

Our definition of God implies that there is an afterlife and that this afterlife preserves the continuity of identity because the absence of an afterlife would either be a limitation on the omnipotence of God or an affront to the love of God. If we, as imperfect earthly parents, can love our children enough that we want to continue our relationships with them even after they have grown up, then we should not presume that God's love for us would allow us to perish. The notion that God loves us but does not care to have us around once our mortal life has ended is a limitation on the expression of God's love and, therefore, should be rejected. As well, the idea that God would allow death to forever separate us from those we love is also inconsistent with belief in a loving God.

It is not enough, however, to focus only on being consistent in our application of the value of love to our definition of God. Because the task is to determine which faith-beliefs work best for the liberation of love, we must take an active role in adopting beliefs that discourage selfishness. As imperfect people, if we do not have a belief in an afterlife, then we are hampered to some degree in our ability to express love. This is not to say that one cannot be a loving person unless che believes in an afterlife, nor should this be taken to imply that all who believe in an afterlife are more loving than those who do not. The point is that, *all other things being equal*, having a faith-belief in an afterlife helps to liberate love. Fear of death is a primal instinct; it has great survival value for any species. Replacing this instinct for self-preservation with a service-motivated attitude not only preserves the value of self-preservation, but also works to keep the value of self-preservation in check when love calls on us to lay down our life for another.

Belief in an afterlife not only helps to liberate us from the fear of death; it also liberates us from fear in general. When an eternity lies ahead in which to redress problems, make sense of that which seems senseless, and vindicate the hope of better things to come, then the future loses the power to promote fear. Trusting in God's plan for the future helps us dissolve selfishness in the present. It encourages us to face each moment as a new opportunity for the expression of love.

Letting Go of Judgment

Recognizing all people as children of God creates the connection that liberates love. Trusting that God will provide for us after death allows us to be liberated from fear of the future. Refusing to spiritually judge others liberates us from the arrogance of presuming to be the arbiter of which children of God are worthy of love.

Judgment is a tricky issue because there is both a spiritual and a secular context in which the word "judgment" gets used. The word *judgment* is similar to words such as *faith, belief,* and *knowledge* in that these words take on very different meaning depending on whether they are used in a secular context or a spiritual context. Secular judgment addresses the *actions* of others; spiritual judgment addresses the *worth* of others. Secular judgment is concerned with determining what kind of behavior is appropriate and what to do about misbehavior. Maintaining healthy boundaries in one's relationships is an act of love, not a withholding of it. Spiritual judgment presumes the ability to look into the depths of another's soul to determine whether che is worthy of being loved. Letting go of spiritual judgment liberates love through acceptance of the precept that judging another is simply not our job.

The appropriateness of exercising judgment—be it spiritual or secular—is based on one's right to be in a position of authority. There are various types of authority, and each one has a corresponding type of judgment associated with it. For instance, we enjoy a cultural appreciation for the personal authority to choose our close friends. The love we have for our friends cannot be coerced. Others may correctly or incorrectly identify our friends, but they cannot pick them for us.

The authority of a judge or a jury is a socially sanctioned authority. The right to exercise this type of authority comes from the power given to government by citizens to orchestrate social relations and to arbitrate private disputes. We can all have an opinion about whether O.J. did it, but we do not all have the power of a juror to exercise that opinion as a judgment. Although sometimes jurors are called upon to make a determination about someone's intentions, this is not a matter of spiritual judgment. The question before jurors is not whether the accused is loveable. Developing beliefs about what a defendant may have done or thought in the past is merely a socially sanctioned system designed for the preservation of healthy social boundaries in the material world. No one presumes that jurors are endowed with the power to see into another's heart; they are simply asked to help make the best of a bad situation.

In an effort to cease judging others, some people adopt the attitude that everyone has a good heart and is doing their best. This position has the value of defining everyone as worthy of love. But when we do this, we destroy the integrity of freewill. To presume that we are always doing our best implies one of two things, neither of which is desirable. Either we are presuming people are perfect in their use of freewill, which eliminates the value of the process of achieving perfection, or we have eliminated the possibility of choosing to be selfish, which in turn corrodes the concept of freewill and takes the glory out of love. The issue is not with the conclusion of this type of judgment, but with the willingness to ask the question.

The question that comes up when anyone steps into the role of a spiritual judge is "Who made you God?" One of the implications of considering ourselves children of God is that we are *equally* children of God. Although older and stronger siblings may sometimes "lord it over" younger and weaker ones, such behavior is never appropriate unless authorized by the parents. Unless we sink to the level of "might makes right," being older, stronger, wiser, or even *correct* does not confer the right of authority. This is why spiritual judgment invites the question: "Who made you God?" and why younger siblings learn how to say, "You're not my boss!" at a very young age.

The refusal to attempt the usurpation of authority strengthens the foundation on which we build healthy, loving relationships. This is equally true for biological family relationships, social relationships, and spiritual relationships.

25

JOIN THE CLUB

✦ ✦ ✦

Human things must be known in order to be loved,
but divine things must be loved in order to be known.
The Urantia Book, p. 1118

✦ ✦ ✦

I have presented three essential faith-beliefs for
maximizing the liberation of love. These faith-beliefs are
1) that we are children of God, 2) that God's love will provide
us with an afterlife, and 3) that we should not sit in spiritual
judgment of others.

It is my hope that we will all affirm these faith-beliefs
and, thus, be united as a spiritual family. I believe that love
and logic lead to this decision, but I cannot *prove* this to you.
There can be no compelling conclusion. Such would be
inconsistent with the Freewill Love Factor.

If you have not yet decided to have faith in God, I
encourage you to take the time to make this decision now. In
the privacy of your own thoughts, search out your heart's
desire to see if being a faith-child of God is okay with you,
too. May we be unified for all time in the belief that we are
the children of God and forever share the love of this glorious
spiritual relationship.

This is what works for me. I hope it works for you, too.

PART VI

USING THE WORD
FATHER FOR GOD

The remainder of this book presumes that you embrace the faith-beliefs outlined in the previous chapter. This means that the language of theism, rather than the language of agnosticism, will be the new language of *choice*. With this change, a whole new world of possibilities opens up for discussion. The possibility addressed in Part VI is the opportunity to pick a name for God that reflects our core values and beliefs about God. To this end a redefinition of the word *Father* is offered which, ironically, is consistent with the feminist critique of language.

TRANSFORMING THE GENERIC GOD INTO A NAME BRAND

✦ ✦ ✦

A rose is a rose by any other name.

✦ ✦ ✦

Theopomorphism looks at reality as a reflection of God's creativity.[7] This art form interprets creation in terms that are harmonious with spiritual values and beliefs and seeks ways to meaningfully express these insights. The following discussion on the use of the word *Father* for God is presented as a way to apply theopomorphism to our core values and beliefs about faith. Although I believe that referring to God as our Father is *generally* the best practice, this, to me, is a lower order of belief than a faith-belief. Spiritual unity comes through recognizing each other as children of God, not through reaching uniformity on how to refer to God.

---

[7]One of my assumptions is that spiritual beliefs should never be in conflict with the discoveries of science. When there is an apparent conflict, either the discoveries of science are inaccurate, spiritual beliefs are incorrect, or both. In terms of creation, this implies that evolution is one of God's ways of creating.

Theologizing about a name for God requires the same objectivity and detachment that was required when philosophizing about whether faith in God is a logical extension of love. There is no room for family baggage on this trip, either. Only the most universal experiences are worth considering in the development of theopomorphic insights. The shortcomings of our parents must not be allowed to cloud our vision of what it means to be a child of God. Naturally, we will project our ideal of the perfect parent onto God. But God's capacities go far beyond our own. If some of our personal experiences help us understand what it means to be a perfect parent, great. If not, we need to let it go.

Because God is everyone's parent, we must explore what is common, *and what we should strive to create as common*, to everyone's parent-child experience. Admittedly, the question of how families should function is a huge topic on which there is a great diversity of passionate opinion. There are many different types of family in today's modern world: traditional nuclear families, families that have experienced divorce, same sex couples, plural marriages, families who have adopted children, to name a few. For the purpose of this discussion, there is only one belief that needs to be accepted to appreciate the logic of what follows. It shouldn't be hard to swallow. It is simply that, *in general*, biological fathers provide a unique and positive value for children by participating in their upbringing.

The name we use to symbolize our relationship with God is important because it is an opportunity to reflect the values and beliefs that we hold most dear. Appreciation for the core qualities of our relationship with God can be nurtured and strengthened by the name we choose to refer to God. Additionally, appreciation for our role as human parents can be uplifted using a word that reflects our idealistic aspirations for familial love.

"Sticks and stones may break my bones, but names will never hurt me," is a principle taught to children in an effort to help them prioritize the relative value of the spiritual, the mental, and the physical facets of life. As a true reflection of the human psyche, however, such an adage is a bold-faced lie. People do get hurt by negative labels and inspired by positive ones. One need only to look to the function of "spin doctors" to understand the effect that the power to name wields. Military, political, religious, and industrial institutions all express the importance of this power through their use of language.

Additionally, many feminist writers have brilliantly critiqued how the power to name can effect social discourse as well as the thought patterns of cultural consciousness. One of the great lessons of the feminist critique of language is the admonition to be personally proactive when faced with language that fails to reflect the progressive march of societal and individual values. It encourages us to not only rename where appropriate, but also to redefine in those instances where an old word has an opportunity to take on new meaning.

By wisely choosing a name for God, we can create a more personal and intimate relationship. A shared meaning for God's name also helps unify those with common faith-beliefs.

Although this section is primarily focused on redefining the use of the word *Father* in the spirit of feminist critique, what follows should not be interpreted to mean that we should stick to just one name for God. Different contexts call for different names. Some contexts call for reference to God's parental love. Other contexts focus on God's power, primacy, or universality. Inasmuch as faith is an extension of love, a name for God that reflects the value of love has merit over words that reflect other attributes. It is in this sense that some names may be "better" than other names. Three core attributes of our relationship to God justify *Father* as the best name for God.

(1) We are children of God.

(2) We share with God the quality of being persons.

(3) We share with God the quality of freewill.

Incorporating these three connotations is important because they provide structure for understanding and living a life of love. These core qualities of relationship provide guidance about who and how to love as well as affirming that we *can* love.

THREE CRUCIAL CONNOTATIONS

✦ ✦ ✦

You only get out of it what you put into it.

✦ ✦ ✦

We Are Children of God

By choosing a name for God that identifies us as children
of God, the fundamental relationships of spiritual life are
reflected back through the archetypal relationships of family
life. Choosing a name with the connotation that we are
children of God serves two purposes. First, it glorifies the
parent-child relationship as a supreme expression of love.
And second, it implies the siblinghood of humanity.

In general and ideally, the greatest expressions of love are
found in the parent-child relationship. The family always has
been and continues to be an institution where extraordinary
levels of care and concern are exhibited over an entire
lifetime. A word for God that carries a parental connotation
can tap into our idealization of what it means to be a human
parent. Using a parental word for God conjures up images of
care and concern that inspire and challenge us in our efforts
to express and receive parental love.

Generosity and mercy are the archetypal forms of parental
love. These expressions of love are appropriate because of

the hierarchical relationship between parents and children. The parent-child relationship gives rise to the sibling relationship. Fairness and justice are the archetypal forms of fraternal love. These expressions of love are appropriate because of the equality of status between siblings. On a broader social level this translates into an appreciation for democratic values. Thus, taking the family as a model provides a foundation for approaching relationships of equality and hierarchy with love. Fairness, justice, generosity, and mercy become glorified as the primary colors of love's refraction through the prism of primary personal relationships.

There are various words that can be used for God that have a parental connotation. For instance, Parent, Father, Mother, and Father-Mother all carry a parental connotation. The next step is to narrow this down by looking at the second key connotation.

We Are Persons with God

Every human being is created through the union of two specific persons. Of the several names for God with a parental meaning, there are only two that also connote a specific person: Mother and Father.

Mother and Father are *personal* names because they carry a personal connotation. All the other words with a parental connotation are conceptual in nature. This category will be referred to as *concept* names. Only the personal names clearly signify that God is a *who*, not an *it*. Concept names are inferior to personal names in the same way that the love of concepts is subordinated to the love of persons. This is what validates rebelling against a democracy that votes in slavery—love for democracy is not an excuse for the inhumane treatment of others.

Of course, painful past experiences with parents to some degree impedes everyone's ability to allow the personal names to engender feelings of intimacy. By refusing to allow such experiences to influence our decision about naming God, we take ourselves a step closer to leaving our family baggage behind.

It's good to nurture the worthwhile experiences that a life of faith can provide. Feeling the loving presence of God is somewhere at the top of the list of worthwhile experiences. The lure of such a wonderful feeling can be a stumbling blocks when it comes to considering faith because it is a selfish motivation, but once the decision is made, these same feelings nurture and nourish faith. *By all means,* let's nurture and nourish faith in every way consistent with love and wisdom. There is no point in opening the door to experiencing the love of God, if we're not going to walk in.

Faith is not merely a willingness to believe a good idea. More importantly it is the willingness to love God. Before faith is chosen, God is only a concept. We distance ourselves from feelings when making a reasoned decision about faith, so that wisdom is not clouded by emotion. But once the faith journey has begun, we should make every effort to be consistent with what we have chosen by *celebrating the joys of the decision.*

The wide variety of ways in which the word *love* is used is unfortunate. We love ice cream. We love our dogs. We love a good argument or good joke, and we love it when our team wins. This word must also find a place in the expression of our highest values and most cherished relationships. The chameleon quality of the word *love* makes choosing a word for God that has a personal connotation all the more important. By doing so, we glorify the personal quality of our relationship with God.

By applying the value of a personal relationship, the variety of words with a parental connotation was narrowed to two choices—Mother and Father. Fortunately, there is a third core quality to consider in choosing a name for God. Incorporating this quality can narrow the field to one option.

We Have Freewill

Love is predicated upon freewill. Belief in freewill makes love possible. Asserting that we have freewill is our best answer to how a self can be selfless. The desire to glorify the belief that we share freewill with God is what narrows the choice down to *Father.*

Even though men and women share equally the quality of freewill on a spiritual level, men and women are not free to make the same kinds of choices on a physical level. Fathers choose to be fathers in ways that mothers do not choose to be mothers. Simply put, a father can be a father and not know it. By having intercourse and then not sticking around to see if a child is born, a man can choose to remain ignorant about becoming a father. It is in this sense that the experience of fatherhood is a matter of freewill choice. Biology eliminates a mother's option for knowing whether she has become a parent. Just as only women exercise maternal choices, men uniquely enjoy a freewill option about experiencing the fact of their fatherhood.

Complementing this freewill choice available to fathers in their relationship to their children is the fact that children must exercise freewill in order to *experience* their father *as* their father. Even though we can teach children to say "daddy" at a very young age, an understanding of the father's role as a creator is beyond their comprehension. Years after they learn to address their fathers with an appropriate name, children develop the level of sophistication necessary to appreciate the role that fathers play in procreation. Then, based upon the *willingness to believe*, they are able to appreciate their fathers as co-creators of their existence. Thus, it is through freewill choice that children begin to relate to their fathers as co-creators.

In contrast, all children experience their mothers as creators, even if they are not developed enough to express this experience or appreciate it with any degree of sophistication. The development of the brain during pregnancy provides children with awareness of their mothers. A lack of sophistication and being in utero form an enormous barrier to a developing child's ability to articulate this experience, but the *experience* of who one's mother is on a cognitive level is nonetheless real. By giving birth and nursing their children, mothers continue to provide children with experiences of the parent-child relationship. The physical nature of this relationship provides an experiential basis of awareness of mother as creator and sustainer of life. But nature does not provide children with a cognitive experiential basis for knowledge of their father. Belief is the common foundation on which children build a cognitive awareness of a father's creator quality.

Comparing our relationship with our biological father to our spiritual father is a natural choice if the goal is to glorify freewill. It is through their willingness to believe that children develop a cognitive experience of their biological father. This is true on the spiritual level as well. Our willingness to believe is the crucial factor. Additionally, biological fathers must exercise their freewill in order to experience themselves as fathers. Therefore, using the word *Father* for God can also carry the connotation that God chooses to be part of our lives.

By redefining *Father* in this way—as a glorification of freewill—we can liberate the word from the critique that its use is sexist, arbitrary, or traditional. Liberation of the word *Father* from its masculine connotations is not only in harmony with, but also is encouraged by, the feminist critique of language. Because freewill is no more a masculine quality than a feminine quality, using *Father* to connote freewill does not need to carry the baggage of masculine attributes. In similar ways, we recognize qualities of motherhood that are not necessarily feminine. For instance, if a father raises a child alone, he is not necessarily considered effeminate for assuming roles more commonly associated with motherhood. Understandably, masculine connotations will to a certain degree leach onto the word *Father* simply because men are fathers and there is not much history of redefining the term in this way (yet). But, by refusing to allow these unintended and unnecessary connotations to trump the use of it, we exemplify commitment to the value of being nonsexist.

When it comes to choosing a word to refer to God, if we have a desire to glorify life's parental, personal, and freewill attributes, logic leads to the conclusion that the word *Father* is the best expression. Who would have ever guessed?

PART VII

EMOTIONS AND ATTITUDE

The purpose of this section is to help re-integrate our emotional bodies with our spiritual life. Just as a surgeon must have the emotional control to not cry over the patient, it was important to not allow the roller-coaster ride of emotions to undermine our ability to think critically about the choice to have faith in God. Now that the logic of love has led us to the conclusion that faith in God best supports love, an appreciation for the role of emotions can take on new meaning and value. Additionally, an understanding of what it means to have a "good spiritual attitude" can serve us well in our effort to make the most of life through faith.

SPIRITUALITY AND EMOTIONS

✦ ✦ ✦

While traveling in India in early 1987 I was blessed by an invitation to visit The Meher Baba Pilgrim Center. I did not know anything about Meher Baba at the time, but being interested in spirituality, I decided to accept the invitation. During my one-week stay there, I learned that Meher Baba devotees believe that Meher Baba was an avatar. An avatar is a periodic incarnation of God. Meher Baba taught that he had previously incarnated as Zoroaster, Rama, Krishna, Buddha, Jesus, and Mohammed.

Meher Baba did not speak a word from 1925 until he passed on in 1969. He communicated by use of a self-styled sign language that his close associates came to learn and by using an alphabet board on which he would point out letters in order to spell words. I was told that he did not speak because he believed all the great truths about God had already been expressed. His mission, therefore, was to awaken people, to inspire people to focus their lives on loving God.

Of the many stories I heard about Meher Baba during my stay at the pilgrim center, my favorite one concerned his appointment of a principal for an elementary school that he had directed his followers to establish. I do not recall the name of the principal. Let's call him Simple Simon because, as the story goes, he could not read or write. Meher Baba had an inner circle of disciples called the mandali. These men were similar to Jesus' apostles in that they worked very closely with Meher Baba and reported to him directly.

When the mandali heard that Meher Baba had picked Simple Simon to be the principal of the new school, they were very distressed. They saw the appointment of Simple Simon as an embarrassment and an administrative nightmare. Some of them took it upon themselves to try to persuade Meher Baba to change his mind.

They pleaded with him for an explanation. "Why? Why would you pick someone so undereducated and unqualified to be the principal of a school?" Meher Baba pointed to a nearby stick and indicated to the mandali that they should go get the stick and hit him with it. "No! No! We cannot do it!" they beseeched him. "We love you with all our hearts. We could never bring harm to you. Ask us anything. But please, spare us from an atrocity such as this! We cannot bear it!"

Then, Meher Baba told them to get Simple Simon. When Simple Simon arrived, Meher Baba told him to get the stick and to hit him with it. Without hesitation, Simple Simon did as he was told. Looking to his mandali, Meher Baba communicated that only those who are asleep disobey, in the name of love, the one whom they call God.

✦   ✦   ✦

Emotions can easily become an obstacle to critical and logical thinking. For this reason, I encourage a dispassionate, though light-hearted, analysis of the issues relating to faith in God. This allows the logic of love to bear fruits that will nourish us for a lifetime. By not indulging emotions, the steadiness of a critical and logical mind is available to safely pilot our souls through the uncertain waters that separate one gnostic paradigm from another. Also, our best hope for unifying ourselves through shared meanings and common values comes from developing a shared reasoning. This, however, does not mean we should deny ourselves the supreme celestial joy that naturally flows from the faith-recognition that we are the children of God. After all, we are not Vulcans.[8]

Emotions have the potential to be an excellent resource for guiding spiritual growth. Emotions, when permitted expression, are the body's way of reflecting *what* we value in life and *how* we value it. They represent the physical integration of mind meanings with spiritual values.

Emotions can generally be classified as deriving from one of three states of consciousness: 1) loving in the present, 2) being fearful about the future, or 3) being judgmental about the past.

Our emotions are like a political system in the sense that it is important to distinguish between the creation of a model system and whether that system is used well. For instance, a well-run democracy could vote for the enslavement of a particular race. This does not mean that democracy is bad; it only demonstrates how a good system can be used to create a bad result. In a similar way, even if we express our emotions in only healthy ways and in appropriate circumstances, this does not mean that we are instantly eligible for sainthood.

---

[8]Vulcans are a fictional race of people from the *Star Trek* series who shun emotions in an effort to glorify logical thinking above all other states of consciousness. Spock (referred to in Chapter 2) was a Vulcan.

In order to have good government, we must strive to improve the mechanisms of government as well as the nobility of the citizenry. In order to live healthy spiritual lives, we must express emotions in a healthy manner as well as attend to the personal enhancement of meanings and values.

Spiritual life is fostered by loyalty to supreme values and an ongoing enhancement of meanings. Vigilantly working for the development of meanings and values helps us wisely direct our *outward* experiences of love. Emoting is the *inward* expression of these value loyalties and mind meanings. When we act (or don't act) in ways that are inconsistent with our values, we are lying to the world. When we emote (or don't emote) in ways that are inconsistent with our values, we are lying to ourselves.

This is not to say that unless every emotion is immediately expressed, we are being untrue to ourselves. Maturity demands that we balance the spontaneous expression of emotion with the demands of living. Emotional disengagement allows the surgeon's hand to remain steady. Unfortunately, for a wide range of cultural and personal reasons, the mere experience of certain emotions is sometimes considered wrong. When emoting in general or when some specific emotion becomes taboo, we lose the ability to clearly see the meanings and values that we attach to life.

Emotions can reveal our current state of spiritual growth when viewed as a reflection of the meanings and values that we *actually* (not idealistically) attach to life. This is equally true for the physical, mental, and spiritual facets of our lives. On the physical level, for instance, a lack of food can create a physical pain. But the pain is not the emotion. If one is fasting for God, the pain of hunger may engender an emotional attitude of repentance that brings forth tears of remorse. If one is starving in a prison camp, the pain of hunger may develop into a fear of death or it may arouse hatred for one's captors. On the mental level, trying to solve a difficult math problem may cause the mind to struggle. This can result in debilitating frustration or be an exciting challenge. On the spiritual level, difficulties with others (or with life in general) may result in a wide range of emotional responses. We may become angry as a result of judging another person. We may feel sad that someone's heart has slammed the door on love. Or we may feel joy born of the hope and trust that from such tribulation greater friendship will develop.

Love begets happiness and sadness because life on earth is imperfect. Love brings the joy of relationships. It brings us pleasure to see those we love do well and inspires gratitude when we appreciate the blessings in our lives. When relationships go poorly, love is reflected in sadness occasioned by a sense of separation. Love may also beget sadness because of our compassion for the suffering of others. In contrast to love, selfishness generally brings about various forms of fear and judgment. Fear is the basis for selfish emotions about the future; judgment is the basis for selfish emotions about the past.

Emotions, when they are neither overly repressed nor overly indulged, are the healthy way in which we become integrated with our values on the physical level. Those emotions that are the product of love should be accepted in the body (permitted healthy expression) and *validated* by the mind. Validated emotions are reinforced as the worthwhile product of the values that give rise to them. In contrast, emotions that are the product of fear and judgment should be accepted in the body (vented in ways that will not make our situation worse) so that we may become aware of our need for a more spiritualized attitude and a greater level of understanding. Such selfish emotions, however, should not be validated. They should not be reinforced by the mind because they are not consistent with our supreme value of love.

By accepting but refusing to validate emotions that are not the product of love, we give ourselves an opportunity to see ourselves (as well as the world around us) in a new light.

Pent up emotions, especially ones based on selfishness, are a vexation to the spirit and an obstacle to the reasoning abilities of the mind. By allowing the body to release these emotions, we are able to let go of unloving attitudes. Once the body has released the tension created by selfish values, then the spirit and mind are once again at liberty to recommit to holding love as the highest value.

3D LOVE

✦ ✦ ✦

When you love love, then love loves you, too.
Bruce Cockburn

✦ ✦ ✦

3D love refers to the process of developing a good attitude through *learning to love learning to love learning to love.* If this makes no sense to you, don't bother rereading it. The explanation is what this chapter is all about.

In order to appreciate an attitude of 3D love, we'll start with the first step: *learning to love.* Taking on the task of learning to love reflects the activation of freewill for a chosen purpose. The purpose is to love others. This is the first dimension of love. Learning to love reflects the recognition that, as imperfect beings, a gap exists between talking the talk and walking the walk. Saying that we hold love to be the highest value is not the same as living that way. Idealism does not make us hypocrites, but it does not make us perfect either, thank God. This gap between our current manifestations of love and our ideals creates the opportunity to work with God in being the architects of our own perfection. Savoring this opportunity is what 3D love is all about.

In order to begin savoring this gift, we must value *learning to love learning to love.* (This is two-dimensional love.) With or without faith in God, the path of love is difficult. People get crucified, shot, and beaten up every day for their commitment to love. This is literally true for some of us and metaphorically true for all of us. One does not have to be a high-profile spiritual or political leader in order to experience persecution for the sake of love. External opposition, however, is the easy part. Added to this challenge is the incessant clamoring of the ego for self-aggrandizement and constant gratification. Put all this together with what was stated in the previous chapter about how love sometimes begets sadness, and it's easy to see why two-dimensional love is no joy ride.

The attainment of a noble character requires loyalty, courage, idealism, trust, and hope. These traits, which are essential for the maximization of love, are not developed without a struggle. Understanding the value of this struggle is at the heart of two-dimensional love. Much of this book has been dedicated to creating this type of understanding. Appreciating the Freewill Love Factor, balancing justice with mercy, embracing the opportunity to be the architects of our own perfection, and taking responsibility for our interpretation of evil are all integral to the process of learning to love learning to love.

But two-dimensional love, the intellectual appreciation of learning to love, does not necessarily provide us with a good attitude. Understanding what is the right thing to do and feeling good about it do not always go hand in hand. As the children of God, we quite naturally seek that inner peace which surpasses all understanding. As a state of being, 3D love is sometimes expressed as laughing through the tears. As a state of doing, 3D love remains calm during a crisis. *Learning to love* learning to love learning to love is what takes us beyond just understanding to feeling good about doing good. 3D love embraces the process of, actually appreciates the opportunity for, learning to love learning to love. This is the best definition I have for a "good attitude." I hope it helps because, in the words of Forrest Gump, "That's all I have to say about that," . . . for now.

Buy One For Yourself
or
Give One As a Gift!

✦ ✦ ✦

ORDER FORM

Please send me _____ copies of *The Logic of Love* at $14.95 each.

Fax orders:
303-530-2582. Just fill out this form and send it!

Telephone orders:
Call toll free: 1-877-HKatzen (452-8936).

E-mail orders:
halbert7@aol.com

Postal orders:
Insights Out Publishing, P.O. Box 11286, Boulder, CO 80301

Where will this book be sent?

Name: _____

Address: _____

City: _____ State: _____ Zip: _____

Telephone: _____

E-mail: _____

Sales tax:
With sales tax, the cost is $15.50 per book plus shipping and handling for orders sent to Colorado addresses.

Processing Charge:
US: $4.00 for the first book plus $2.00 for each additional book.
International: $7.00 for first book plus $4.00 for each additional book.

Payment:
❐ Check   Credit card: ❐ Visa ❐ MasterCard

Card number: _____

Name on card: _____

Exp. date: _____

ABOUT THE AUTHOR
✦ ✦ ✦

For over twenty years, Halbert Katzen has been refining his unique insights regarding spiritual life, family life, and social structure. He is engaged in a three-book project, addressing these topics, respectively. Each book generates a paradigm based on holding love as the highest value in one's life. Additionally, Mr. Katzen writes article length pieces on spiritual and social issues. His ability to present this multifaceted material in an easily understood and enjoyable style comes from a combination of formal education and life experience.

While attending Brandeis University, he created an interdisciplinary major called *The Nature and Development of Religious Experience.* This work combined the perspectives of anthropology, sociology, and philosophy with his interests in theology. He also attended the University of Colorado in Boulder, receiving a law degree and an MBA.

As a spiritual educator, a legal professional, and an environmental and political activist, Mr. Katzen has developed his skills as an effective public speaker. He has been a guest on the Denver talk show, *Spiritual Spectrum*, and lectures on a variety of subjects relating to spirituality and family structure.

How to Contact the Author

Halbert Katzen is available for speaking engagements and individual spiritual counseling. He may be reached at:

Insights Out Publishing
P.O. Box 11286
Boulder, CO 80301

Toll free: 1-877-HKatzen (452-8936)
Local calls: 303-530-9508
Fax: 303-530-2582
Email: halbert7@aol.com